Why I Never Lie
And 19 Other Mostly True Stories

Why I Never Lie
And 19 Other Mostly True Stories

Rick Cornish

Word Sower Publishing

Copyright © 2011 by Rick Cornish

All rights reserved. This book or any portion thereof may not be reproduced or used in any manner whatsoever without the express written permission of the author except for the use of brief quotations in a book review.

Author portrait by Lynn Cornish
www.lynncornishwatercolors.com

Book cover and interior design by Michael Sharps.

Printed in the United States of America

First Printing, 2011

ISBN: 978-0-9834474-3-6

Word Sower Publishing
www.WordSowerPublishing.com

This book is dedicated to my wife Lynn, who has enough spirituality and no-holds-barred honesty for the both of us. And more than anyone else, the book was written for my three grandchildren, Ava, Ted and Lexy, (and, of course, all who may come later), in the hopes that they'll know a little more about their gramps than he did about his grandads.

Preface

On November 11, 1956, I decided I would be a writer. I'm certain of the date because at my elementary school Parent/Teacher Night was always the Wednesday night before Thanksgiving, and in 1956, when I was in the third grade, Thanksgiving was on November 12. (God bless the Internet.)

I laid awake in my bed listening to my mother and father debrief their ten minutes with Mrs. Nelson. As usual their hushed whispers got louder and louder as the conversation wore on.

"Did you hear," my mother said, "did you hear? 'Fifty-dollar words'. She said Ricky uses 'FIFTY-DIOLAR WORDS'."

"Yeah, I heard. I also heard he still can't read."

"That's not so. That is NOT so," my mother argued. "He's just slow to take up reading. We already knew that. But did you hear Mrs. Nelson, she said he can PRINT faster than he can read."

"That," my father said, his voice raising, "isn't saying much. Have you seen Ricky print? And it takes him longer to READ? For Christ's sake."

"Well, he uses fifty-dollar words, and Mrs. Nelson says no one in his class can say nearly as many big words as him. She says when he tells stories in class, everyone leans forward and listens. His teacher says he's a natural born storyteller."

"Great," my father snapped, "He can't READ stories so he makes them up."

And that, as they say, was that. My dad didn't know it at the time, of course, but he'd pretty much summed up the rest of my life. In the fifth grade I'd write a piece for our school newspaper about a softball victory that, with it's 'fifty dollar words' made it into the local newspaper, (thankfully the Hayward Daily review wasn't strong on fact-checking)....'Highland Slaughters Markham in bloody massacre'. In the seventh grade I'd write a social studies report on the South American Slugamaguchi River that would win the praises of our home room teacher, Mrs. Bowers, and then soon after result in an unscheduled parent-teacher conference when Mrs. B. learned there was no such river. In high school I would balance my D's in math and science and all the other courses with my A's in lit class. And by eighteen I'd have my first free lance writing job, one that helped finance my four years of undergraduate college, writing biographies of famous dead people for five bucks a piece. In my sophomore year at Chabot Junior College I would finally convince the girl I was chasing, and who would eventually become my first wife and the mother of my two boys, to go out on a date with me instead of staying home to write a book report, which I would write for her, ('The Incredible Jazz Age.....Ten Years of Excess'; written completely from whole cloth), and which would earn Claudia an A. Then at San Jose State I would morph from a D student to an A student once I was able to take all lit and writing classes, and by my first year in grad school I would win a short story competition that would get me into the creative writing program at San Francisco State. Although I only attended three classes before dropping out, I was set to begin a career as an author.

And the fact is I really did live my dream. For a year or so. Then I was offered a 'real' job by one of my freelance clients….good money, excellent benefits, paid vacation, job security….and for the next forty years instead of short stories I wrote research reports, proposals, contracts, memos, speeches, long-range plans, responses to Grand Jury investigations, by-laws and policies and…well, you get the picture.

Now I'm retired and I have begun what a friend calls 'act three'. Time to get back to story telling. I truly hope you'll enjoy these mostly true stories.

Contents

Why I Never Lie	1
My Dog Phil	17
Hunters and Gatherers	25
What Buffalos Are	31
Thank you Howard B. Stark	47
Shakespeare in the Rockies	51
Junk	59
New Year's Eve with Buck Owens' Bus Driver	79
Just About Four Seconds Flat	87
Broken Crown	103
The Rock	117
Almost Banjo	137
I Like to Cook A Lot A Lot	143
No Experience Necessary	153
Cello's Map; A Cautionary Tale	167
Plan C	185
Why I Type So Fast	205
The Nancy Waiver	213
Cornish Miners	217
The Rescue of Albirdio	225

Why I Never Lie
March 2004

I'm an honest person. But there was a time in my life, when I was young and eager to impress, that I sometimes stretched the truth. Nothing big, just a little exaggeration here, a little white lie there. Okay, even an occasional whopper. But "What could be the harm?" I figured. And then I found out by nearly getting myself whacked. Let me explain.

Famous Estates Illustrated was a book, actually a series of books, used by estate planners and attorneys to sell their services. It was a book about famous (and not so famous) very rich dead people. A financial planner would sit with his wealthy client, open the book to, say, Louis Armstrong and there, on two opposing pages, would be a big photo of Satchmo, a brief biographical sketch of about 350 words, a summary of the terms of his last will and testament and a breakdown of all his estate's assets, probate settlement costs and the bottom line—how much dough his family got. 'See there, Mr. Jones, Armstrong's assets were about the same as yours and look…see there, the estate was raped by state and federal taxes. Now, we can do a lot, lot better than that.'

Not exactly great literature, but the year was 1971, I was fresh out of college, and I had a degree in English that, according to my parents, was real close to no degree at all. And, of course, my sole ambition in life was to write the great American novel. Making a living writing anything, even something as grimly dry as Famous Estates Illustrated, was light years better than checking groceries at Albertsons. So when I was offered some freelance work—traveling around the country researching probate files and microfiching obits at local libraries and then returning home to write up the profiles--I concocted a scheme. The owner of Famous Estates paid precious little for the research and writing, but he was more than generous when it came to paying expenses, which would include air travel from one city to the next and all lodging, food and incidental expenses. But I'd hitchhike and only fly the long hauls, stay in flea-bitten motels instead of nice hotels and eat lots and lots of Big Macs. With the money I'd save in expenses, along with what I'd make researching and writing, I could afford to write biographies of famous dead people half the time and the great American novel the other half of the time. I had a plan.

To get the hang of it, I did a local trip first and drove my '56 VW Bug to San Jose, San Francisco, Oakland, Sacramento and then down to L.A. On each trip I'd visit the probate court first, collect information on twenty famous dead people (Jack, the owner, furnished me with a hit list) and then go to the local library and photocopy obituaries. It took me a little over four weeks to knock out seventy-five biographies, seventy-five "Will Highlights" and seventy-five "Probate Abstracts". (This was about a week longer than I'd planned, but I figured the more I did, the faster I would get—which is what happened.) Then I spent two weeks working on my novel (which amounted mostly of sitting in front of my IBM Selectric typewriter wondering what in God's name I was going to write about. (Thirty years later and I still haven't figured that one out.)

My first real research trip, the trip on which I learned never to make up stories, was to the east. I flew to Boston, then hitch-hiked to Providence, took the bus to New York City, then hitched a ride to Philadelphia and finally to Lancaster, PA. From there I'd head home via a Pam Am flight from JFK back in New York. Before flying off to Boston I'd never been out of California except a few times to Tahoe and once to TJ. I was twenty-two, traveling alone, actually a freelance writer and I was tasting life for the first time. It was one of the truly great times of my life. There were huge adventures, life-changing experiences, crazy, crazy people in each of these cities…the two or three days spent in each town could be an entire story by itself. But I'll tell this one.

I'd been on the road just short of two weeks when I was dropped off at Exit 231 on Interstate 78 just outside of Lancaster; Amish country, but none were in sight. It was a warm summer afternoon, I was on the home stretch and I was happy as a clam. I pulled my back pack on, adjusted the strap, and I walked the half-mile into town. I'd already decided that I would stay in a decent hotel my last two nights on the road and, coming into Lancaster's main street, I spotted a four story Holiday Inn towering over the rest of the buildings. It was a clean, nice little town, nothing like the big cities I'd just come from, and the street was bustling with activity. As I approached the hotel, I could see a knot of people gathered on the sidewalk in front. There was a white news van with a TV broadcast antenna on top—WLTV—ALL THE NEWS YOU NEED TO KNOW.

"Sir, sir, what do YOU think of the news?" A young woman holding a microphone and wearing a miniskirt had grabbed my shoulder and turned me toward the camera. I was on TV.

"What news?" I asked.

"Spiro Agnew, the Vice President of the United States, has just resigned from office."

I let out a yelp and danced a little jig.

"Can we assume," the reporter asked, "that you welcome this news?"

"Welcome? WELCOME? Are you kidding, this is a great day for the U.S. A GREAT DAY." I yelped again.

"And why is that?"

"Because Spiro Agnew is a crook, a money-grubbing, dishonest politician of a crook who should never have been elected in the first place. And because his resignation brings us one step closer to the big guy who'll be taking a tumble next."

"President Nixon?"

"Oh yes indeed, ma'am, President Richard M. Nixon. Millhouse Nixon. Yes, yes, yes." I was ecstatic. I danced another jig.

"And sir, let me ask, what you do?"

"Do?" I asked.

"I mean, for a living? Are you just passing through?" She was eyeing my backpack.

"Oh, yes, passing through. I'm a freelance writer. Here in Lancaster doing some research. For a book." Man it felt good to say that.

"Oh, really, what sort of book?" The camera was still rolling.

"Well, ah…." And this, dear readers, is the point at which you meet the real me in 1971. The superficial, eager to impress twenty-two year old with oh so much to learn.

"Well….it's ah, it's sort of an EXPOSE' ", I said, instantly regretting that I'd lied. Actually, I regretted it in less than an instant. A nano-instant.

"Really," the mini skirted reporter exclaimed stepping closer. "And what will you be exposing in our fair city?" I could smell her perfume now.

"You know…..the usual. Corruption, graft, ah, general scandal type stuff. Can't really say more than that." My voice trailed off and I just stared blankly at the reporter. The next moment she was interviewing someone else. Mine had been about thirty seconds of fame, not fifteen minutes.

My room at the Holiday Inn wasn't a room at all. It was a palace. My beds, two of them, were the size of regulation snooker tables, there was a television that actually worked, with a remote control that worked and the TV was color. And best of all, I had my own personal, completely unshared, clean bathroom. After nearly two weeks of bare light bulbs, cracked plaster, floral-patterned linoleum floors and the unrelenting fear of the dreaded bed bug, I was back among the living. I showered, put on decent clothes and went down to the hotel bar.

"Scotch rocks," I told the bartender, loving the way that sounded. Scotch rocks. The Holiday Inn lounge was full, it was the end of the workday and apparently this was one of the downtown after-work hangouts. A minute later I had my drink and was just taking my first sip when the woman sitting on the bar stool to my right nudged me.

"Hey," she said, "isn't that you?" She pointed at one of the ceiling-mounted TV's. I was dancing my jig of joy there on the sidewalk, my huge, bright orange backpack heaving up and down on my back.

"And what's that on your back?" she asked.

I told the woman my story, truthfully, briefly and with no embellishments. The bartender listened in, and so did the guy on my left.

"So what's this book about that you're writing? What's all this scandal stuff about anyway?" asked Johnny, who was pouring me a drink, this one on the house. I could see others in the lounge were listening now and I suddenly had a sinking feeling in my gut.

"Oh, it's just some stupid book, boring, really…legal, financial stuff. Nothing anybody would wanna read. It's just…..ah….some stupid, boring book. A book about probate law. Booooor-ring." I wasn't trying to hide anything, it's just that it really was a stupid, boring book and trying to explain Famous Estates Illustrated to a bunch of half-lit strangers in a bar seemed like a stupid, boring thing to do. Looking back, I believe now without reservation that there was nothing I could have said at that moment that would have been greater proof that I was in Lancaster Pennsylvania to write a simmering, explosive exposé. A piece designed specifically to point fingers, to get someone in trouble.

When I emerged from my hotel room the next morning, I was transformed. I'd arrived in town in dirty jeans and tennis shoes and an orange backpack. As I walked businessman-like down Main Street, Lancaster PA, I was in a pin-stripped shirt, madras tie and corduroy sport coat. And I was carrying a brief case, not wearing a backpack. Half way to the county courthouse I was stopped by a Lancaster Observer roving reporter who wanted to know what I thought about Agnew's resignation. No, it's true. I swear, it's true. I told him what I thought, briefly (no dancing this time). He took a head shot with his camera. The young newspaper reporter, about my age, asked me my occupation. I told him free lance writer….that was it, nothing more.

"Oh, right, the "Expose' Guy". Caught you on KLTV last night. Hey, man, how about that Darlene Love. Is she one righteous chick or what?" He was speaking of the perfumed reporter, of course. I was beginning to feel cursed.

At exactly 8:00 a.m. I was at the steps of the courthouse when the guard opened the doors and, by 8:45, I was pouring through files and feeling better now that I was back in the grind. The clerk allowed me to take three packets at a time (each containing every single scrap of paper concerning the probate of one of my subjects, one of my famous dead people), and when I was finished with them, she had the next batch waiting for me. I was making good time. If this kept up, I thought, I could finish by noon tomorrow and head back to New York early. I decided I'd take the train instead of hitchhike.

But when I went back for my third bundle of files, the old woman behind the counter only had two. "Where's Donavan?" I asked, "Daniel Donavan, where's his file?" "Oh," she chuckled and rolled her eyes, "you'll need to come with me for the Donavan file. This way." I followed the old clerk down a hallway, up one flight of stairs and into a room about the size of a broom closet. "This," she said, pointing at scores of three inch thick files bound in manila covers with two-hole metal binders that were stacked neatly on metal shelves that reached floor-to-ceiling on three of the four walls, "is Mr. Donavan's probate file." The woman turned to leave but then, as an afterthought, said over her shoulder, "We close at five."

I'd experienced this a few times on my research trips…..probates that involved such vast wealth and were embroiled in such contention and legal turmoil that they could go on for years. Even decades. And the longer the probate case was open, the more paper was generated. (The classic was a case involving an Atherton, CA pretzel heiress who left three hundred and twenty million dollars for the care and feeding of "squirrels and other small pastoral creatures. That one's probably still in the courts.) Finding the few tidbits of information I needed to write my profile would be like finding a needle in a haystack. I handled this in Boston, and again in Manhattan, by simply skipping the giant files and going down further on Jack's hit list. But I couldn't do that this time. Daniel Donavan, city father, land developer, millionaire fifty times over, was the main reason I'd come to Lancaster. Jack wanted Donavan's profile in Famous Estates Illustrated and I couldn't go home without it.

By closing time I'd found what I needed in the Daniel Donavan probate file, but I still had well over half my subjects left to research. I'd blown the entire afternoon on one file and, instead of leaving early the next day, I might not get to leave at all. The next day was Friday, which meant I'd have to spend the weekend there, which meant I'd have to find the Lancaster YMCA, if Lancaster had one. I went back to the Holiday Inn and headed straight for the lounge.

"Scotch rocks," I said, feeling far, far less clam-like than I had the day before. When the bartender returned with the drink, I reached for my wallet.

"Here, let me get that." A man, well dressed in a dark Italian suit and Italian shoes, had sat down on the stool next to me. He looked to be about forty. "Put it on my tab, Johnny," he said to the bar keep. "Sure thing, Mr. Bella."

"Hi, my name is Salvatore Bella," he extended his right hand. "And you're the young writer from California, here to write about the wild goings on in our little burg. Rick, isn't it?" He had a firm grip.

"How do you know me," I asked with surprise, but then instantly knew. We both laughed.

"TV….newspaper, you're famous, kid. Hell, you should run for office. Like Spiro, eh?" He laughed again, and this time Johnny the bartender laughed with him and so did I.

Tony and I sipped our drinks and talked. He told me he was a real estate agent, had lived in Lancaster most of his life but had secretly always wanted to be a writer. A novelist.

"I admire you, Rick. A young kid, traveling the country, writing books. What a life, what an adventure. Tell me about what you write."

"Well," I said, warming up to the chance to talk about what really mattered to me, "mainly I've written short stories…had a few published. But right now I'm working on my first novel. I'm just at the outline stage at this point, but I'm beginning to see the characters. You know, they're just now coming into focus."

"So you're here in Lancaster researching your novel? In probate court?"

"How'd you know I was at the courthouse today, " I asked.

"Saw ya there, hunkered down over some papers. Seems like I spend half my life there filing papers. I'm a realtor, remember?" Tony ordered us another round.

"Oh yeah, right. No, I'm not working on my novel here in Lancaster. I'm doing a free lance job…..collecting material, then I'll go home to write it all up."

"Boy, now that sounds interesting. That's the kinda thing I could get into." Salvatore lit a cigarette. "So what kind of material are you collecting exactly, Rick?"

I told Sal, (I was calling him Sal now), about Famous Estates Illustrated, about how the book was used to sell estate planning, about how I traveled around doing research and then how I would write up the little profiles, even about how I used my expense money to support my creative writing. When I finished, Sal Bella stared directly into my eyes without saying a word. It was as if he was trying to look past them and into my mind. He just stared, his expression blank. It gave me a little chill.

"Well," he said finally and stood up. "It was good talkin' with ya, kid. Good luck with your book and all." And he was gone.

That morning, at around 2:00 AM, there was a loud rap on my hotel room door. "Bell hop", came a voice from the hall. I jumped out of bed, pulled on some trousers and opened the door. Sal Bella and two other men came into my room and closed the door.

"Get dressed, someone wants to talk to ya," Tony said without the least bit of threat or menace in his voice.

"Hey, man, what's this all about. It's two a……."

"Get dressed. Now! No talkin'" A little menace this time. I started dressing quickly and in silence. The two men with Salvatore were both much bigger than him, both well over six feet, both heavy set, both in dark suits and ties like Bella.

When I was dressed Sal motioned to my open brief case on the desk. "That your research stuff?" he ask. I nodded. "Grab it," he said, "and let's go."

The four of us rode down the hotel elevator without a word spoken. It was a long, long ride. I could hear my heart pounding. I found myself hoping that someone would be in the lobby, but it was empty. Parked on the street in front of the Holiday Inn were two shiny black Lincoln Town Cars. Sal opened the door to the back seat of the car in front and told me to get in. When I hesitated, one of Sal's two guys stepped toward me. I got in, sat down, the door slammed and the car screeched away.

"How do you do, Mr. Cornish, my name is Frank Moretti," said the man sitting beside me in the back of the Town Car. It was dark and I couldn't quite make him out, but I could see that he, too, was dressed in a dark suit.

"Hello," I said. I'm pretty sure my voice cracked when I spoke.

"Mr. Cornish, let me get right to the point. I have a friend who works in the Hall of Records downtown and he told me that you spent the better part of the day going through the probate files of a fella by the name of Daniel Donavan. Why are you interested in Donavan and his estate, Mr. Cornish? And what is your affiliation?" It was a curse. I knew for sure now that it was a curse, and I'd brought it on myself.

"Affiliation?" I stammered.

"WHO DO YOU WORK FOR?" It was Sal in the front seat and menace was now definitely in the mix.

My mind raced. I didn't want to bring Jack into this. Into WHAT, I asked myself. If I told him Jack's name and these guys called him and…….

"AFFILITATION," Morretti said. "NOW."

"I work for Jack Hanley, a publisher back in California who produces a series of books called Famous Estates Illustrated." My mouth was dry and I had trouble getting the words out.

"And what is Famous Estates Illustrated and what does Danny Donavan have to do with it?" asked the man in the shadows. For the second time that day I explained the book, what my job was and why I was in Lancaster. "To be honest, sir, I don't know why Jack included Donavan on the list of subjects to research. I'm assuming it's because his estate was so large….about sixty-five million I think."

"More like eighty. Sonny, I gotta tell you, I'm just not buying any of this crap you're feeding me," Frank said.

"Well, ah, let me show you the book. Can I show you the book?"

"What?" asked Frank.

"Famous Estates Illustrated. Can I get it out of my brief case? I carry one with me on research trips to show probate clerks I'm on the level. Can I show it to you? Please?"

"No, keep your hands out of the brief case," said Sal, "keep them where I can see 'em." "Give me the brief case."

As I handed the briefcase over the seat to Sal, Morretti told his driver to pull over and stop. Sal and his boss got out of the car with the briefcase and walked back to the other Town Car, which had been following us. I glanced back and saw Morretti get in and the console light go on. "Eyes straight ahead," barked the burly driver scowling in the rear view mirror. My head snapped back and I didn't move a muscle.

It was fifteen minutes before Frank returned to the car and got in. He handed me my briefcase and told the driver to return to the Holiday Inn.

"It was the girl, right? The reporter," Frank said.

"Huh?", I said.

"You made up the baloney about the exposé to impress the pretty TV reporter. Right?"

"Ah, I guess so."

"You guess! He guesses, Sal," Morretti and Bella and the driver all laughed.

When we pulled up to the lobby of the hotel, Mr. Morretti told me to give him all of the notes I'd made while going through the Donavan file.

"Okay," he said, taking the three or four sheets of paper from me. "Now I've got three things to tell you, kid, and I want you to listen real, real good. Number one. Don't write nothing about Danny Donavan. Forget you ever heard the name and tell your boss back in California to do the same. Number two. Don't ever tell anybody about our talk tonight. NOBODY. And number three, don't ever make stuff up. It can get ya in a lot of trouble. And besides, women ain't worth it. You understand?"

"I understand," I said and got out of the car.

And that's why I never lie.

My Dog Phil
September 2007

Mildred White, which is what we called my aunt, (my mother was named Mildred too, and this avoided confusion), was always in her dark bedroom with the shades pulled down. She'd been in a sick bed ever since I could remember. For my entire remembered life, my aunt had been slowly dying, shut in her shadowy, stuffy bedroom with the covers pulled up tight. I never asked what Mildred White's illness was and was never told. Now there's no one left to ask. Grandparents, mother and father, aunts and uncles (nearly two dozen of them), sister, all gone.

It was on a Saturday morning in the summer of 1970 that my father called me from Hayward to say Mildred White was going to pass soon. "If you want to see her, you'd better come up here today." He knew I would want to see my aunt. She and my uncle Lloyd had lived across the street from our house, and I'd had closeness with her that came from talking, there in her darkened room, from the time I was a little, little boy until I was an adult. Most days I would go visit Mildred White and my grandma and we'd talk, sometimes a few minutes, sometimes an hour, and we'd always manage to make one another laugh. Sure I wanted to see her one last time.

So that sunny summer morning Phil and I drove the 45 minutes from San Jose to Hayward in my little black Volkswagen. Phil was a two-year-old mostly Dalmatian and he went most places I went. For being barely out of puppyhood, he was exceptionally well mannered, mostly, and was very patient. He would sit in the front passengers seat, alert and upright on his haunches, and every now and then he'd lean his head out the window and his big ears would flap in the wind.

Mildred White looked terrible. She would surely be dying soon, I thought as I entered the room. My grandma, Maude, was sitting there on the edge of the bed, talking with Mildred White. As they had since I was a little boy, the two made a fuss over me, and then over the dog.

"Oh mercy, mercy, mercy," my grandma feigned horror, "look at that beard. Oh, mercy me. If that beard doesn't make you look the spitting image of that drunken Grant, then, little boy, I don't know who on earth it does." My grandma always called me "little boy" and always said that about my beard; it was playful and loving but it carried its intended disapproval. My grandma hated my beard and she hated Ulysses S. Grant, a contemporary of hers in the same way that Harry Truman, who died when I was little, was a contemporary of mine. My grandma was from Kentucky.

Mildred White agreed weakly in a whisper, "Yes, Mama, it sure is the general's beard, and this boy is getting tall as a tree." The two of them loved me so much—of course, because they'd watched me grow from a baby to a grown man, my aunt living just across the street, my grandma living in a cottage in our back yard. But there was more to it than that. Maude had had eleven children in all, and among all those kids my dad had the only son. (There was one other, Little Harold, my uncle Red's son, but he'd been killed in his late teens when I was just little. Murdered. But that's another story.) So of all the cousins, I was the only male to carry on the family name.

"Hurry now," Mildred White said, "get that moose of a spotted dog into the room and close the door." She was afraid that Phil would upset her Pomeranians. Mildred White always had a few Pomeranians around the house and they were always getting upset about something. It used to be me and the bugs, worms, spiders and occasional small animals (usually rodents) I would bring to share with my aunt and grandma. Now it was my dog.

Once inside and with the door closed I sat down opposite my grandmother on the bed and, after a small amount of sniffing (Phil was not interested in these Pomeranians) and two or three tightly walked circles, my dog laid down on the hardwood floor and dozed off.

My grandma looked tired and drawn and very, very old, which of course she was. And I knew she'd been crying. Her daughter, her only daughter out of eleven children, would soon be gone. And Mildred White.....well, Mildred White lay in her bed, as she'd lain most of my life, but she looked different now, almost as if she were already in her casket.

But it wasn't a sad time we had that summer morning. Not at all. We talked for a good long while, probably longer than we'd ever sat and talked. Mainly what we three did when we were together was to take turns telling stories. I remember that Saturday morning my grandma told our favorite story, one we'd heard many, many times, of the last Blackfoot raid in the Nebraska Territory. She told of how her mama had taken her, her two sisters and her brother down into the root cellar where they had stayed for three days and three nights. And how my great-grandma would sneak out each night and feed the chickens and the hog and the geese. No Black Foots ever came to their sod hut, but it was still our favorite story.

Mildred White retold the tale of how, twenty years earlier, Uncle Cyrus had walked all the way into Hayward for a hair cut one morning and had come home that afternoon, a little more confused that usual, with a Mexican prostitute whom he said he would be marrying, "after I talk to her pappy." And about the time my father went to buy a hog at the livestock auction in Russell City, got drunk, ("boiled-as-an-owl" she said), with his pals and returned home with a burro for my sister and me instead. I watched as my aunt choked the story out. Her eyes were sunken into her skull and the color of her skin was gray and a little yellow and utterly lifeless. She was coughing a lot, especially when she got to the funny parts and we were all laughing. "And Millie (my mother) said, 'You damned fool, those kids need a dunkey like they need a hole in the head. You take that damned dunkey back right this minute. And don't come home without a hog.'" The three of us laughed a lot that day.

It was quite a while before Phil let it be known that he was running out of patience. Probably close to two hours went by before he got up from the floor and began pacing in front of the door, his nails click-clicking on the hardwood floor. I pretended not to notice and he just laid down and fell back to sleep. This was a special time for Mildred White and my grandma and me and I wanted to think that somehow he knew it. It had been a few years since we three had had a chance to be with one another alone, without the rest of the family. (I'd grown up and gone away to college.) And we all knew it would be the last time.

I told Mildred White and my grandma about how I'd just won a short story writing contest at school. Of course they wanted to hear all about the story so I told them, remembering the narrative almost verbatim. They were both delighted. Both were avid readers, both valued the written word, both knew that my dream since early childhood had been to write professionally, and both believed that someday I would amount to something.

Phil got up again, walked over to the bed and looked me in the eyes. There was no ignoring him. "Okay," I said sternly, "in a minute. Now go lay down." My spotted dog went back to the door, clickety-click, and flopped down with a deep sigh.

"Oh mama, tell Ricky what little Harold brought you," Mildred White said, sitting up in bed just a little and smiling, her dim eyes brightening for an instant. Little Harold was one of a bushel of second half-cousins, a blood relative but just barely. He was a bizarre twelve year old who, in later years, would become an even more bizarre man. But again, another story.

"Well, he brought me a dead mouse."

"A dead mouse? Why in hell would he....." I was laughing so hard I stopped to catch my breath.

"Come on, let's go," Phil said.

The dog had awakened and he was now looking at the three of us. We couldn't speak. I looked at Mildred White, she looked at my grandma, and they both looked at me, our eyes locked, but we couldn't speak. Phil stood up facing the door and then looked back at us over his shoulder. If it is possible for a dog to look irritated, Phil looked it. I looked at my watch. We'd been there for three hours.

Finally my grandma spoke.

"Did you hear that?" she asked no one in particular. "Did you just hear that dog speak?" I nodded first, then Mildred White, after several seconds of hesitation, also nodded. The room was silent except for the tick-tock of a wind up alarm clock on the bed stand. We sat for at least two minutes, maybe more, without a word, the humans staring at the spotted dog, the spotted dog staring back.

"Well, I'm gonna go," I suddenly said, springing up and giving both women a quick peck on the cheek. "Mildred White, I'll be back for a visit before too long. You get feeling better."

Of course she didn't get feeling better and died soon after that last visit. Only once my grandma and I spoke of the talking dog. It was at the wake after my aunt's funeral. "Ricky," she said in a hushed, tired voice, "it's best that we don't talk about this to anyone. Do you understand? Do you agree?"

"Yeah, I understand, and no, I don't plan on telling anyone. But, grandma, what do you suppose happened? How did that…ah… did it happen?"

"Oh, little boy, it did happen all right. As sure as I believe we put my girl in the ground today I believe it happened. But why or how I just don't know. Maybe Mildred White knows. Isn't it nice to think she does?"

My dog Phil went on to do many undog-like things in the two short years that we had him, but never anything nearly as undog-like as talk. Not before and not after. He was such an uncommon dog that my wife and I decided to name our first son after Phil the Dalmatian. (In retrospect, it was a good decision. Phil the son has gone on to be a very uncommon human.)

I waited seven or eight years after my grandma's death before I told the story of my talking dog to another living soul. The living soul, a close friend, didn't believe it. But that's okay; I know it's true. I was there.

Hunters and Gatherers
July 2004

In my late twenties I stumbled, literally by accident, onto bluegrass music, when, from the instant I heard Jake Quissenberry and the Lost Ramblers sing a straight-ahead, hard-driving version of 'Little Maggie' at a bluegrass festival my pal John Bunch and I mistakenly had driven four hours to attend on the faulty assumption that a "bluegrass festival" was actually a BLUES festival with a healthy heaping of cannabis, I was hooked for life. Sitting there on a log at dusk, surrounded by the tall ponderosa pines at the Nevada County Fairground, Friday, June 17th, 1976, everything changed. I would learn to sing and play bluegrass (first guitar, then bass and finally fiddle), I would form a bluegrass band that continues to perform thirty years later, I would introduce my son, Phillip, to the music, which led to his becoming a remarkable singer/songwriter/picker, I would become active in the California Bluegrass Association (CBA), eventually becoming the chairman of its board of directors, (a development that bespeaks the co-dependent enabler role taken on at the early age of six years old), and most importantly in the grand scheme of things, I would make countless dear and lifelong friends.

It's worth noting that up until my introduction to bluegrass and its practitioners and fans pretty much one hundred percent of my friends shared my political, social, religious, and philosophical tenets. That is to say, they were all liberal, Democrat, progressive, agnostic existentialists. (Well, that last might be a stretch, but at the time I certainly wanted to believe they were.) Once bluegrass music happened, all that changed, almost overnight. The folks I met and with whom I played music, began hanging out and eventually mingled into my life….and these folks were all over the socio-political-spiritual map. How can that happen? How can you suddenly become friends with a person whose belief system is contrary to yours? Well, you can't. What happens is this—bluegrass people don't talk politics or religion. Over time you begin to discover that some of your new friends, while not belonging to the same political party, or the same religion, are in most other ways, and if you're lucky, important ways, just like you. This is the story of one such friend, one of my closest.

It was on a Saturday morning at Hollister's Good Old Fashioned Bluegrass Festival that I had the good fortune of wandering by the camper of Tim and Sue Edes just as they were sitting down to breakfast….and the even greater fortune of being told Tim had cooked too much. (It's always an accident when I run into Tim's camp just as he's about to eat.) Over eggs easy-over, fried potatoes and a steaming, glistening mound of bacon, we three chatted for maybe ten minutes before the rabbit incident came up. Sometimes it takes longer, sometimes even less time, but sooner or later, we re-tell the rabbit story; it helps a little if someone who's never heard the rabbit story before is there, but that's not a requirement.

The story begins on a cold and stormy night, the wind is howling and I'm walking through sheets of rain in a grassy parking area at the Yolo County Fairgrounds looking for Tim's rig. It's the CBA's annual Veterans Day Festival, fourth and final, (it only took us four years to figure out that late November was not a great time for an event that included camping). There are a couple of dozen or so campers in the field, it's pitch black, not a trace of moon, and I'm just about to give up looking when I spot Tim's pick-up and cab-over camper. I rap on the door, it opens and I come in out of the cold and rain. I'm cold but thankfully dry. Tim pours me a glass of wine.

I didn't know Sue very well at all at the time, but she and I hit it off right from the start. Tim and his wife and I talked for close to an hour in the warmth of the camper, gusts of wind occasionally shaking it on its wheels, fierce ran pounding the roof like so many machine gun rounds. Finally I pulled on my heavy down coat, thanked the Edes for their hospitality, opened the door and then quickly slammed it shut.

"My God," I said, "there's a rabbit out there."

Tim thought it was a joke. "Oh, so you're afraid of rabbits in the dark now.….put that in your candidate's statement next year for the CBA board election. Rick Cornish —INTEGRITY…. LEADERSHIP….And did we mention a furry animal phobia?"

"No, really man, there's a rabbit out there on the ground and it's alive but hurt. It's moving. And I can see red. I'm sure it's blood."

"Let me see," Sue said squeezing by me and opening the camper door. She slammed it shut too.

"He's right, honey. There's a little rabbit out there and it's hurt and bleeding. You've got to do something."

Tim looked at me impatiently, and then at Sue.

"So what do you want me to do, Sue, give it mouth to mouth?"

"Get out there Tim," I chimed in with a chuckle, "and save that little critter's life. And wash up before coming back in. Could have rabies." Sue glanced at me and wasn't smiling. So much for our blossoming new friendship.

"Tim, seriously, you've got to go out there and put that poor little animal out of its misery. Just shoot it."

Tim looked at his wife pleadingly. "Honey, I didn't bring a gun, what am I gonna kill it with?" There were a few moments of silence. The wind howled outside….the lights in the camper flickered, but just for an instant.

"Well," I said after a long moment, "I noticed a shovel leaning against the camper. Couldn't you just, ah, you know, whack it?"

"Couldn't YOU just whack it?" Tim snapped back. An even longer silence followed. Maybe two friendships in jeopardy.

"I don't…..ah…..or I haven't…..ah…..killed…..ah…..things. I mean, living things. Well, insects, of course, and a bird with a bee-bee gun once, but that was on accident. It was a horrible experience. But never anything with fur.....you know.....like a mammal." They just stared at me, I think in disbelief. Tim was a life-long hunter, an honest-to-God outdoorsman, and Sue was married to one.

The wind wailed outside and the camper shook. For a moment I thought I could hear the rabbit moan. (Do rabbits moan?)

Sue finally broke the silence. "For God's sake, honey, just go out and whack the bunny."

"Yes, Tim, whack the rabbit," I chimed in.

"I don't WANT to whack the rabbit. I'm a hunter. I shoot things. I don't beat them to death with a damned shovel......Are you even sure there's a rabbit out there?" Now Tim looked out the door.

"Daaaaaamn," he droned, closing the door and looking for his boots. "Daaaaaamn!"

Pulling his yellow slicker on, Tim made one more protest. "I really don't get why it has to be me," he said, even though he was now clearly resigned to handling the 'situation'.

Tim sighed, stepped out of the camper and closed the door behind him. I was relieved he'd closed the door, and I was pretty sure Sue was too. Neither one of us wanted to watch. Once Tim was gone, Sue looked at me. "Well," she said, "you know, people fall into one of two groups—hunters or gatherers. You and I are gatherers, and Tim, he's a hunter."

"I'm definitely a gatherer," I nodded.

Moments passed in silence. In less than a minute Tim returned holding an empty white plastic bag. "SaveMart" was written on it in brilliant red.

"Here's your bunny," Tim sneered.

Okay, there are variations on the story depending on who tells it. But the facts are the facts. And I'm guessing that when I see the Edes at the next festival or camp out, we'll re-visit that night at the Yolo County Fairgrounds.

What Buffalos Are
March 2004

I first became aware of my need to own a buffalo as an indirect result of a silly little argument with my wife, Lynn. We were having lunch at the Hong Kong Café on Main Street in Sonora and we both ordered chow mein with egg foo yung. When our lunches came, my foo yung was more or less round while Lynn's was more or less square.

"Trade me," she said, "I'm not really that hungry. I want the smaller portion."

"Smaller portion? They're the same portions, one's just round and the other's square."

"No," Lynn said, "yours is smaller than mine."

I explained to Lynn about measuring area….how if the perimeters of two objects are the same, they can have different shapes and they'll still have the same area; I told her this in the least patronizing voice I could muster. Lynn said I was wrong. We debated. I'm happy to say that this type of disagreement is generally about as bad as our arguments get anymore.....one of the nice by-products of a long marriage.

Nonetheless we debated. She said that, to determine the area of an irregular shape, you'd need to break it into triangles. I said you'd need simply to determine the perimeter and then apply a mathematical formula. She asked what formula. I said I didn't know but that I was sure there was one.

"Look," I said, "I could go home right now, walk off the perimeter of our pasture and in a matter of minutes, know in square feet the exact area. You think we can put men on the moon and not be able to figure out the area of egg foo yung?"

"I didn't say that. I said you can't do it with just a perimeter."

Lunch ended and we were at an impasse. Which was okay, because neither of us cared much.

Except, of course, being who I am, I couldn't let go. That afternoon, while Lynn was out on an errand, I measured one of my strides with a tape measure and then walked off the perimeter of our pasture, multiplied the steps by 34 inches and, presto, I had the perimeter measurement. It only took me fifteen minutes, and since the whole area was bounded by a wire fence, it was easy. The next step would be a snap; I just needed to get the formula to apply to the number. For that I called my good friend, Dick Todd, a surveyor, civil engineer and banjo picker with whom I played music.

I told Dick about the debate at lunch and finished off with the number of feet I walked off around the pasture. Dick just listened.

"Okay," I said, "what's the formula."

"Well," my friend replied, "you've got roughly 3.2 acres of fenced pasture."

"Okay, but what formula did you use to get that? What's the magic calculation? I can't wait to show Lynn."

"Rick," Dick said with a long sigh, "there IS NO magic formula. Lynn was right. You were wrong. You cannot calculate the area of an irregular shape by simply applying the right geometry to the perimeter of a shape. Didn't you take geometry in high school?"

"But we sent a man to the moon, dammit. And you're telling me we can't figure out….wait a minute. If there's no formula, how do you know the acreage of my pasture?"

"I looked up your Whiskey Creek parcel on the County Planning web site while you were telling me your story. I'm doing some consulting for them and they gave me a password. Great satellite shot; I could pick out your llamas."

"No magic formula?"

"None. If there were, we surveyors could play a lot more golf."

"And you say 3.2 acres?"

"Right," Dick said. "You know, your pasture is under-utilized with only two llamas and two goats. You could easily run more livestock in there."

I explained to Dick that the concept of "utilization" was not really an operative one in the Whiskey Creek context because: 1) We didn't shear the llamas to obtain their wool for spinning, nor did we use them for pack animals; 2) we had no intention of eating our Boar goats, even though Boar goats are "meat" goats; 3) we didn't milk our goats because, as fellows, they're not the milking kind; and 4) the original "utilization" plan I'd had, which was keeping the weeds down in the pasture, had been set aside when Lynn discovered the various designer hays, grains and pellets she could buy for her pets, Gwen, Claire, Joe and Ted.

"So you see, Dick, we don't under-utilize the pasture. We don't utilize it at all, unless you think of it as a gigantic play pen for my wife's pets."

"Well, I'm just saying if you wanted to put more animals in there, you could."

"Duly noted," I said. "Was he nuts?" I thought? As far as I was concerned we had four too many pasture animals as it was. However, two separate events, one week after the area calculation argument, were to change all that.

My youngest son, Peter, drove up for a visit and, as usual, Saturday afternoon he and I went grocery shopping and then to the video store. (We both love cooking, and we both love movies.) Pete picked out the movie—American Buffalo--volume 1 of the "Red

Road" series. Haven't heard of it? Me neither, but Peter was insistent. It was a cult film, he said, French, 1993, a must see.

"Now let me see if I've got this straight. It's set in the American plains, about American Indians, and about American buffalos, but it's made by a French film company in 1993 and it's got sub-titles."

"Yep."

So after dinner Pete and Lynn and I watched the buffalo movie and it was terrible. Worse than terrible because of the sub-titles with which I just can't seem to get traction. Fifteen minutes into the film I gave up on the plot (not sure there was one) and just watched the cinematography which, I must admit, was pretty good. Hundreds, no, thousands of buffalos stampeding one way and then another, and of course getting shot and killed in droves by the cunningly cruel white men all speaking in perfect, wild west French.

That night I dreamt about buffalos. I was driving from Jamestown to my office in Stockton, through the hills, and I came around a corner and there, in the middle of the road, stood a gigantic bull buffalo, just kind of looking off into the distance. I honked, and when he wouldn't move, I pulled over, got out of the car and urged him off the road. I took hold of one of his horns and just sort of gently guided him over to the shoulder. He gazed softly into my eyes….he seemed appreciative. There was kind of a communication between us. I got back into the car and drove to work. It was a nice dream.

The next morning Peter and I drove to Murphys for breakfast—Lynn had housework to do and chose not to go along. Seated in a booth at the Flip-Jack Inn, Peter and I sipped coffee and waited for our omelets.

"Hey, check this out," Peter said handing me the Buy and Sell Press he'd been leafing through. "A buffalo calf, and for cheaps."

I read the add—"Two buffalo calves. Good blood line. All shots. $450 each. Amador County. Call Amos Amos at 209-435-6675."

"This is absolutely amazing," I exclaimed, "incredible. I had a dream about a buffalo last night. It was so real."

"Not surprising given the movie we watched before you went to bed," my son said a little dryly.

"But don't you see, Pete? First the movie, then the dream, now the ad in the Buy and Sell. And I didn't even tell you about my conversation with Dick Todd last week. He says our pasture is underutilized. Hear that? UNDERUTILIZED!"

Having known his father for twenty-five years, my son was fully aware of what was coursing through my mind as we sat there at the Flip-Jack Inn. He knew that, already, in just a matter of a few seconds, I was speeding down the track and he knew too that, once started, there was very little that could stop this train.

"Have you talked with Lynn about this?" he asked.

"Of course not, I just thought of it. But she'll love the idea. Petey-Boy, we're gettin' a buffalo." Peter started to say something, thought better of it, and sipped his coffee.

My wife's love for me is deep and abiding, it's true and it's tender. But it's not, I was to learn that night, unconditional.

"Yes, you heard exactly what I said. But let me say it again. If you bring a buffalo here, to my home, you and that buffalo will be finding another place to live."

I was shocked. Lynn loved animals. Her whole life was centered around them.

"But just explain why….just tell me why," I pleaded.

"You mean again. Okay, I'll explain again. Buffalos are huge, gigantic. They're not pets, they're nothing like a pet. Can you imagine what a buffalo would eat? How much money feeding a buffalo would cost? And they'd walk right through our pasture fences, I'm certain of that. And probably not even notice they did. And can you even imagine what trying to get them back into the pasture would be like? And why bother anyway, because they could just turn around and walk right through the fence again. And what would they do to the other animals? To my llamas and my goats. Buffalos are more like elephants than cows. Don't you understand that?" In all our years of marriage, I'd never seen such adamancy. She was dug in.

"Well, sure, we'd have to do some research and I….."

"Don't bother to research unless you also do some research about a new place for you and your buffalo to live."

"Did I tell you what I was thinking of naming him if, ah, we were to get a buffalo? Bill. How's that for a great buffalo name?"

Lynn sat impassively. No expression on her face. Cold. Conditional.

We were at an impasse, but I figured I had time on my side. I was on that track and, if anything, I was speeding up.

Three days after the last buffalo talk with Lynn, I went in for a teeth cleaning at Dr. Benbow's office. I once read that dentists have the highest suicide rate of any profession and that the reason for this is that they know people hate coming to see them. Sure, on a cognitive, rational level, dentists know that their patients don't hate them personally….but on the emotional, non-cognitive side, according to this article I read, they feel lonely and isolated and, well, hated.

I don't know if my dentist, Dr. Benbow, feels hated, but I know that he's a world-class pleaser….a pleaser like no other I've ever known. He wants to be liked, craves to be accepted and will do or say pretty much anything to win you over. Want more nitrous, doc. Hey, no problem! Tired of sitting in the chair. Sure thing, let's wrap up and we'll finish this up next week. Hate the Niners! Love the Niners! Take a position on something and, once Doc Benbow knows what it is, it's his position too. Good dentist though.

His practice is located on the upper floor of an old, rickety Victorian on Washington Street in the heart of old Sonora—with its mix of forties and fifties vintage office décor and dental paraphernalia, it's an eccentric little place, eccentric like the doctor. My dentist met me at the door, squeezed my hand and led me to one of the two tiny exam rooms—the one with the nitrous oxide. I'd told the doctor on my very first visit that I would need nitrous (laughing gas) whenever I came there….if I came in for a root canal, a teeth cleaning, a consultation….if I just stopped by to drop off a coffee cake for Christmas, I would need nitrous. Dr. Benbow said he understood, and as he guided me into the antique dentist's chair, he flipped on the "N", as he called it. I guess because I'm bearded and usually go to the dentist dressed "comfortably" (that is, in shorts, a tank top and sandals), the doc thinks of me as a throwback from the hippie sixties.

"Here," he said, adjusting the nitrous mask on my nose, "this'll get ya off." And I had no doubt it would—the good doctor was generous with his nitrous oxide, at least when I was in the chair.

"So how are you? Haven't seen you for a while. I'll just get these old choppers cleaned up in a jiffy. I've been fine. Very busy. Daughter's fine. Crazy around here. Busy, busy, busy. No rest for the wicked. Hmmm….open wider. Crazy schedule. Brush more. Floss. Wish things would slow down. Beautiful weather, though, not that I can enjoy it stuck in here all day. How about that Bush. That war. So anyway, how have you been?" That's how Dr. Benbow talks…. rapid bursts of non-sequiturs. Kind of a shotgun approach to conversation, mostly in one direction.

"Wellllllll," I said, waiting for his hand to exit my mouth and then for a momentary break in the nitrous induced fog that was now building in my brain, "trouble with wife. Won't let me….. buy…..buffalo."

"Well, now, that seems unreasonable," said the doctor predictably. "You've worked hard all your life and should have a buffalo if you want one. As I recall, this is the same wife who wouldn't let you have a tractor. Is that right?"

I nodded and grunted yes, my brain no longer able to form even short sentences.

"Personally I'm a big fan of buffalos. Always have been. Majestic creatures, and very historical. And good eating, too. Why, I remember once when…..What's your wife's objection?" (When he got on a roll, Dr. Benbow even interrupted himself.)

With every ounce of concentration I could muster, I struggled to get the words out—"too big….break fences….hard to con…. con….contrabullon….

"Hard to 'control'?"

I struggled through the fog to nod.

"Hmmm," said Dr. Benbow. "It surprises me to hear that your wife would have those kinds of concerns. What I know of buffalo just isn't anything like that. Ah, in fact, my neighbor, he keeps a buffalo right there in his pasture with his horse and two llamas. These buffalos you buy nowadays, they're nothing like the animals you read about in the Old West. Why, in modern times we're talking 'hybrid' buffalos, much smaller, more like cattle. And very accommodating like cattle, too. You don't really need anything more than a wire fence for these critters. And my neighbor's trained his to come when he calls it. Very tame. Why, I remember one day….." Dr. Benbow rolled on, his bucolic narrative, along with enough nitrous oxide to calm a bull rhino, or a bull buffalo, creating beautiful pastoral images in my slowly melting mind…..

green rolling hills of great succulent grass, buffalos and llamas and boar goats romping like children, Lynn and I, holding hands, watching from a knoll….all done in soft pastels.

When we were all done and I'd breathed enough regular oxygen for the fog to roll back out, I asked, "So doc, you say you have a neighbor with a buffalo? Who is this guy? Can I contact him?"

"Huh?"

"Your neighbor. The one with the buffalo and two llamas."

"Oh, ah, no," Benbow said. "He's moved. Gone. Moved to, ah, Utah last year. Miss him and his animals. Nope, the neighbor's moved away. But I'll tell ya, those buffalo, they're fine pets. Very loyal, too. You tell your wife I said so."

I couldn't wait to get home. Lynn was unmoved at first, but slowly I chipped away at each of her arguments, one by one, using the ammunition given to me by my dentist. No, buffalos weren't really all that big. No, they respected fences, and besides, they really had no more interest in wandering away than any other pet. And if they did, you just called them back. And they were docile, gentle animals who did what they were told. Despite my semi-conscious state, I hadn't missed a detail.

"Alright," my wife finally said, "but only one. You went off for a goat and brought two home. One buffalo."

"One, I swear." I was excited.

That night I found the Buy and Sell with the buffalo ad and called Amos Amos. Naturally I assumed the 'Amos Amos' was a typo, but when an old man answered and I asked for Amos, he said, "This is Amos Amos."

"Hi, Mr. Amos, my name is Rick Cornish and I'm interested in buying one of your buffalo calves. I was wondering if…."

"Four hundred and fifty" the old man interrupted, "you want it, you come 'n get it." He sounded angry.

"Okay, but I was just won……"

"You want it?"

"Well yes, I….."

"Then come 'n get it. 12556 Old Morton By-Pass, four miles out of Rail Road Flat. Come tomorrow. Noon." Amos Amos hung up. I'd planned on quizzing him about the ins and outs of raising buffalos…..sort of verify what my dentist had told me…..but I figured that could wait till I met Amos the next day in person.

A brief word of explanation is required before going on. I've always loved the way buffalos look. I read that W.C. Fields once said, 'Women are like elephants. They're nice to look at, but I'd never want to own one." Now I realize just how misogynistic the quote is, but I mention it here not because of the reference to the woman but rather because of the point Fields is making about elephants. They are great to look at, terrific to look at, but most people would stop there. And that's what buffalos are—great to look at but maybe not worth the trouble of owning. Except I felt differently. You see, the thought of having a buffalo of my own, in my own pasture that I could gaze upon any time I liked was, well, entrancing. That's the only word for it. Could there be some inconvenience involved? Probably. Was having a buffalo grazing just outside my window worth the effort? Absolutely. I was on a one-way track.

The next morning I drove to Sonora Rentals on 108 just above the Junction. The young woman behind the counter was sipping her first coffee of the day, but when I asked her what type of trailer she'd recommend for hauling a buffalo, she put her cup down.

"You need to haul a buffalo? A real buffalo?"

"Well, actually just a calf," I said.

"Let me get the owner......."

As my old '75 Ford pick-up groaned up the steep grade toward Rail Road Flats, I guess I should have been wondering why the guy back in Sonora had rented me such a massive trailer, (I mean, it was only a calf), but I wasn't. Instead I was marveling at the absolute beauty of the morning, the tall, thick pine trees, the morning sun creeping up over the high peak before me. And I was marveling at how good life was, and how much better it would be when I returned home with Bill. Yes, he'd be called Bill, and he'd join his friends Gwen, Claire, Joe and Ted in a pasture of high green grass and sheltering old oaks.

I pulled into the little hamlet of Rail Road Flat about 10:30 and decided to cool my heels at Billie's Rocket Café until a little before noon, when I'd drive the remaining four miles to the Amos Amos spread. (I guessed it was a "spread" anyway.) Billie's was about half full and I could have sat in a booth, but I chose a stool at the counter.

"Coffee, please. With cream." A middle-aged woman with bright red hair and lips painted bright red to match (I was guessing she was Billie—she had a Billie look about her) poured my coffee and pushed a small stainless steel pitcher of cream down the counter to me. Since moving up to the mountains from the city, sitting in small, backroads cafes had become something I'd learned to enjoy. I sat reading a copy of the Union Democrat and listened to the conversation going on all around me.

I hadn't been there more than ten minutes before I caught the name, 'Amos Amos' coming from one of the tables. Five locals sat in front of mostly empty breakfast dishes, drinking coffee and taking turns telling stories. One old guy, with gray stubble and a broad grin on his face, was just finishing a good one....

"So the young feller says to him, 'Mr. Amos, sir, you wrote right here that the reward was two thousand dollars. See, right here on this poster.' So old Amos-Amos he says, 'Let me see that, boy," and he takes the piece of paper from the feller and he tears it up and he throws it on the ground." They all howled, even the red-haired waitress laughed from behind the counter.

"Then what happened?" one of the men asked.

"Well, Amos Amos he gives the kid a ten dollar bill and says, 'Boy, alls you did was close the damned gate and then come fetch me. If you think yer gettin' two thousand bucks for closing a damned gate, you're dumber than that stump over there.'" They all laughed again.

When the waitress came over to refresh my coffee, I asked her about the story.

"Oh, Stan was just telling the story about Amos Amos and his infernal buffalos for the umpteenth time," she said.

"Buffalos?"

"Yup, a local man here, Mr. Amos, went out and bought him a small herd of buffalo about three years ago, twelve of 'em I think. Was gonna start breedin' 'em on his ranch just outside of town."

"'Was' going to? What happened?" I asked.

"Well, Amos Amos built a fence around his pasture, made it out of timbers sunk in concrete, six feet high, took him a couple months and Lord knows how much money. You'd of figured that fence could 'a kept a herd of elephants penned in but, hell, one day about a year after he got 'em, one of the beasts, the bull I heard it was, just walked right through the fence. Like it wasn't even there. And the rest followed."

"So what happened," I asked, not quite sure I wanted to know.

"The buffalo, they just walked away. For nearly two years the herd just pretty much went anywhere it wanted. Got into people's gardens, trampled fences, ate feed put out for cattle. Amos Amos called the county for help and they said, 'No, they're your buffalo, you brought 'em up here, you catch 'em.' So Amos Amos put up a reward, two thousand dollars, but still nobody could bring 'em in. You ever seen a buffalo up close? They're like a Coors beer truck with legs. And mean." The red-haired waitress made a face. "So finally this young kid, Denny Weaver, is out tending his dad's cattle and the whole herd of buffalo walk right into a small feed pen and start munchin' on the alfalfa put out for the cattle. Denny slams the gate shut and goes for Mr. Amos. And that's how he got 'em back. And you can bet he got rid of 'em right quick after that. May have one or two left, I dunno."

Driving back down the mountain from Rail Road Flat I remember feeling philosophical about the whole buffalo thing. There was no feeling of disappointment; in fact, I was feeling pretty fortunate—I'd been spared what would undoubtedly have been one of the major nosebleeds of my life. And, too, I was wondering if burros and llamas got along well. Oh, and I found myself looking forward to the next afternoon when I'd be going to Dr. Benbow's for my new crown—we'd have a serious talk about his neighbor's buffalo.

Thank you Howard B. Stark
September 2003

As I look back over my sixty-plus years it's plain to see that music has been a potent catalyst in my life. It's brought me together with people I'd never have known, it's taken me places I'd never have visited and it's given my soul a voice it might never have had. I've played, I've sung, I've performed and I've found solace in my music for nearly half a century. And none of this would ever have happened had it not been for Barbara. Or Howard B. Stark. Let me explain.

The summer of my fifteenth year was a season of firsts for me: my first real job, a summer gig at a candy factory; my first "set of wheels", a 305 Honda Superhawk; and my first true love, Barbara, with hair the color of spun gold, eyes bluer than the sky and braces that could light up a room. By the end of summer those three firsts would ultimately combine to lead to two others….my first broken heart and my first musical instrument, which I quickly used [employed?] to sing about my first broken heart.

The Howard B. Stark Candy Wafer Company, headquartered in Evanston, Illinois, didn't make candy wafers in its tiny Oakland plant; it made candy cigarettes. Great long mint candy strings, stretching over thirty feet on a conveyor belt and then chopped into cigarette-sized pieces and painted at one end to simulate the burning ember. My job that summer was to clean off the caked-on sugar that was encrusted on virtually everything in the plant. This was the special job that was saved all year long just for the summer help. I worked hard for close to three months and made enough money to pay off my motorcycle and, by the end of summer, managed to save up enough money to buy my girlfriend a special birthday present—a gold chain costing the incredible sum of $65. SIXTY-FIVE DOLLARS!

When I arrived to work at the candy cigarette factory on the last day before school started, I learned that my foreman, Buck, had saved the best for last. I would be cleaning out the giant stainless steel silo where the sugar was stored. Emptied just for the occasion, the storage tank was three stories high. Stripped to the waist, I was strapped into a harness and lowered into the huge chamber by rope. Next, my colleagues up top lowered a bare light bulb swinging from an extension chord to light up the silo. And there I dangled, like a Christmas tree ornament, chipping away at the hardened sugar stuck to the sides of the tank with a common garden shovel. Nothing high tech here. The air was thick with a fine, sweet dust, suffocating, and the temperature inside the silo was well over one hundred degrees. Buck and the boys pulled me out once, for lunch (no twenty minute morning or afternoon breaks at Howard B. Stark). I spent a very long day in sugar hell, but my spirits were high. I'd be returning to high school the following Monday. And that afternoon I'd be presenting my sweet

Barbara with her gold necklace, which I'd picked up from the jeweler just the night before. If they wanted to dangle me, let 'em. I'd be out of there by five to see Barbara, and I wouldn't be back.

The ride back to Hayward from Oakland on my motorcycle was exhilarating….after being confined in the sweet and sweltering silo all day, the freedom of the road and the cool rushing air felt wonderful. I went straight to Barbara's house (she lived in a posh, gated neighborhood—Woodland Estates—where the well-to-do families lived), hurried up the brick steps and rang the doorbell. Barbara's mother answered. "Yeeees?" It was more a statement than a question. She looked horrified. Repulsed. "Barbara's not home." She closed the door. As I walked back down the brick steps I turned just in time to see Barbara and two of her girlfriends peeking out of a big picture window. And I saw my reflection. I looked like a human-sized glazed gingerbread man. The powdered sugar in which I'd floated all day had stuck to my sweaty body and then, on the motorcycle ride home, the cool air had hardened the sugar. I was completely white and sort of shimmery all over. I just hadn't realized it in the excitement of rushing to Barbara to give her her gold chain.

I got on my motorcycle and rode around for a while. I could feel the caked on sugar coating now, and I could still see Barbara peering out of the window, an expression on her face not unlike her mother's. Then I rode to the jewelry store and returned the gold chain. Sixty-five bucks. Walking back to my Superhawk I passed a storefront—Sherman and Clay Music—and there in the display window was a four-stringed baritone ukulele. Sixty-five bucks. I walked right in and bought that uke. To this day I don't know why. I'd never played a musical instrument, never even thought about playing one. That night I sat up late and learned a

G chord and then a C chord and then a D chord from the little instruction book that came with the baritone. And I learned my first tune....Goodnight Irene.

Sometimes I live in the country
Sometimes I live in the town
Sometimes I take a great notion
To jump in the river and drown.

Shakespeare in the Rockies
December 2003

This is the story of the best summer of my father's life. I believe it's a true story because as I was growing up, and even into my adulthood, he told me the story many, many times. And each time not a single detail ever changed and, during every telling, his voice was full of the same wonderment and delight.

My dad's name was Vance but he was called Bebe (as in BB gun….another story) all his life. Bebe was born and raised in a sod house on the flat and hostile Nebraska Plains. One Saturday morning in the Spring of 1928, he, his nine brothers, one sister and his mother rode their buckboard into town for supplies—they did this once each month. The family was third-world poor, stamps poor, pre-any kind of social services poor. Bebe's father, an alcoholic itinerant preacher and abuser forty years my grandmother's senior, managed to make it back to the homestead every eleven months or so until the last of the brood was sired.

The family scraped by with a truck garden and some chickens, a dollar here and a dollar there made by the older brothers doing odd jobs and by my grandmother's taking in sewing.

It was in the general store of the tiny Plains town of Marshall, in southwestern Nebraska, that my grandmother, Maude, was approached by two men that Saturday morning. Both were strangers to the town, both wore full beards and looked to be in their early thirties. They wore clean, modest clothes and appeared to be working men. One of the men told Maude that they'd seen her ride into town with her young-uns and that they were interested in hiring one of the boys to work for them for the summer. They explained that they were silver miners, headed to their stake in the Colorado Rockies for the season, and that they were looking to take along a boy who could prepare their meals and keep the cabin "clean and proper".

"We'll pay a hunnerd," said the man called Bob, "fifty now and fifty when the boy returns in the fall. And we'll be good to 'im, ma'am." Bill, the other man, nodded.

It's impossible to know exactly what was racing through my grandmother's mind there in the little general store at that moment. She loved her sons and her daughter as much as any mother could possibly love her children. And, to be sure, these were two strangers, rough-looking men about whom she knew nothing. But one hundred dollars could guarantee there would be food on the table for several months to come. And, too, letting one of her sons go with the men for the summer would mean one less mouth to feed, though she shuddered at even thinking such a thing. But Maude knew that it was not uncommon for miners to hire cabin boys during the summer months—the time that mines could be worked in the high Rockies was very limited by crushingly harsh winters, and bringing along a youngster to do light chores enabled the miners to focus their efforts on what was important….finding and extracting silver.

So, Maude agreed. And there was really only one of her sons who could go. The boys older than Bebe all had odd jobs on spreads neighboring the family's small plot of land. My dad was twelve, too young to do heavy ranch work but old enough to keep a wood fire going, cook and clean up. Buford, nick-named Red and the hell-raiser of the nine, was only eleven months younger than Bebe, but sending him was out of the question. Lord only knows what mischief Red could get into, and he surely wouldn't do a lick of work once he got to the mountains. No, Bebe would be the one to go.

When my father came to this part of the story, he always used the same words to describe the scene. "They put me up on the tailgate of that old Model T, wedged in between the boxes and sacks, and off we went. Mama was cryin' hard and so were the younger kids, especially Millie, my little sister—I was her favorite. But for me, it was the happiest day of my life. I spent my whole damned life on land that was as flat as we was broke, but now I was headin' for the mountains. The Rockies."

It turned out that Bob and Bill were on the level, mostly. They did have a cabin in a remote part of Chaffee County, Colorado. At more than 14,000 feet elevation, their silver stake looked down upon the rich green of the Upper Arkansas River valley. The closest town, Leadville, was about sixty miles southeast, but the road up the mountain to the stake was so steep and rough (actually little more than a trail in some spots) that it could have been six hundred miles. The cabin, a large, single room of rough hewn logs, was situated high up on the side of a steep canyon, and Bebe loved it that, no matter where you looked, the ground went either up or down, but was never flat. And he loved the spruce and pine trees. Why, he could see more trees just looking out the cabin window than he'd seen in his entire life back home in Marshall.

Bob and Bill treated the twelve year-old well, just as they'd promised Maude they would. In just a few short days, Bebe had established a routine, one that was quite to his liking. An hour before dawn the boy would be up and preparing breakfast for the two men….fried eggs (the miners had brought three hens along) fried side pork, biscuits and gravy and strong coffee. (And of course after the men left the cook got his breakfast too—Bebe couldn't remember a time in his life when he'd eaten so well…..and so regularly.) While Bob and Bill ate their morning meal, their cabin boy would prepare their lunch and pack it in a tin bucket along with two bottles of root beer. After the silver miners left for their day's work, there were the usual chores….make the beds, sweep the cabin floor and front porch, clean up the breakfast dishes, maybe wash some clothes or occasionally go out to shoot and clean some squirrels for dinner. But by ten or so, the work was done, with nothing to do till it was time to bake bread and start preparing dinner. And that's when Bebe started the best part of his day. He would read Shakespeare.

Going to school wasn't something that any of the ten Cornish kids did much of…and certainly not with any regularity. Bebe had gone pretty steady till his twelfth year (after returning from Colorado he would not attend school again until he was sixty-two and enrolled in a junior college California history class—"for the hell of it"). Some of the kids went a little more than Bebe, some a lot less. But Maudie and her nine boys and her only girl, my aunt Mildred White, were all readers…..voracious readers. Somehow she'd always been able to lay her hands on books, even during the toughest of times; the "fried dough" times, my dad would say, and there was always something around to read in the low-slung sod cabin. Pickings were a lot slimmer that summer in the mountain cabin, but Bebe discovered the first week that Bob was a reader too, and he told the boy to help himself. One book, about three inches thick and leather bound, caught Bebe's attention right off— The Complete Works of William Shakespeare. He'd heard that name, heard his mother say it, and he instinctively placed some sense of importance on it. So the twelve year old decided to read the Complete Works of William Shakespeare, cover to cover…. and he was determined to finish it by the end of his summer in the Rockies. The first play, a comedy, was "All's Well that Ends Well" and Bebe loved it once he'd gotten used to the strange way people talked in those days. (I must confess here that his son the lit major never, ever got used to it.)

And so it was a wonderful and warm summer of easy chores, majestic mountain views, terrific, ample food and William Shakespeare. No back-breaking work like on the farm, no endless competing for blankets with his brothers during cold winter nights, no worrying about whether mama would be able to put food on the table the next day. And Bob and Bill were okay, especially Bob. They'd take off before dawn and come back to the cabin after dark. And they rarely yelled at him. Once, when he'd discovered that he'd forgotten to pack their root beers into the lunch pail and tried catching up with them on the trail down to the mine, Bill had whacked him one in the mouth. "Boy, don't you 'member what we told ya the very first day you come here? We said, 'Boy, you stay at the cabin, or you can hike up the canyon, but you don't never come lookin' for us DOWN the canyon....down at the mine.' You 'member that boy? You BETTER 'member that elst one across the face ain't all's you'll get." But that was only once. Mostly Bob and Bill were good to the boy, mostly they just let him alone.

So the summer wore on, the days were hot and the nights could turn frightfully cold. Bebe continued on through the Complete Works, alternating between comedies, histories and tragedies. By late August he was up to Titus Andronicus. One especially hot afternoon he lay on his cot reading about the Romans, imagining himself there, in the palace, the emperor, surrounded by his scribes and tribunes. He read on, half dozing, when suddenly the door to the cabin thundered off its hinges and splintered into a thousand pieces on the cabin floor. The boy looked up, blinked and rubbed his eyes, and when he opened them again the room was full of men. Four men. All dressed in dark suits and ties and wearing white straw hats. And all holding guns. Big black Tommy guns. He recognized them as Tommy guns from photos he'd seen in newspapers….. photos of G-men.

And that's just what they were. Government Men come to capture and arrest Bill and Bob for making bootleg whiskey in their non-existent silver mine. They hadn't been miners at all. When the two small-time bootleggers returned to the cabin that evening, they gave up without a fight. Before being hauled away to an awaiting black G-man car, Bob tried to give the boy the second fifty dollars the men had promised Maude, but one of the G-men snatched the money away and slipped it into his vest pocket. "That's evidence," he snarled.

The boy was put into the back seat of another black sedan by himself and by late afternoon the next day he was in Denver. The

G-men drove him directly to the train station and there he was put onto a train. By himself. "You just sit here and mind yourself" one of the men said. "The conductor will tell you when to get off. And you consider yourself lucky to be alive and going home, boy. Those two men you were with are desperados. You hear me? You understand?" My dad nodded yes, but he didn't believe the G-man. He felt sorry for Bill and Bob. And he felt bad about going home without the fifty dollars. But still and all, it was the best summer of his life. "To this day," my father would always say at the end of the story, "that was the best damned summer of my life."

Junk
March 2004

Doing the right thing isn't always easy, but doing it after you've done something really wrong can be downright difficult. And complicated. I learned that lesson the hard way during a long, and especially hot, summer in 1960. How hot was it? I remember walking to school our last day before summer vacation and seeing a plastic Santa Claus Christmas ornament on the sidewalk that had melted in the sun. For nearly forty-five years I've wondered how hot it must have been for that Santa to melt….wondered, too, about why it was on the sidewalk in June in the first place. But I digress.

Brooks Judd, my best friend, and I were walking home one day from the Hayward Plunge and we met up with a friend of ours, Gary Richards. We three lived in the Hayward Hills (called the "Highlands"), which meant that to get home we needed to walk up the "Hill", about a mile stretch of road that was very, very steep. Once at the top, the road leveled out into a lesser incline, but getting up the Hill, especially on a scorchingly hot day, was murderous.

Brooks and I liked Gary okay, but we hadn't seen him much in the past year or so, except at school of course. We used to go to Gary's house to play, especially during the summer months, but then, when we were in the fourth grade, Gary and his dad were in a serious car accident. They'd just started down the Hill in the Richards'' 51 Plymouth when the brakes went out. Mr. Richards had to turn the car hard to the right and up an embankment in order to stop—the Plymouth rolled over. Gary was okay, but his dad hit his left temple, smack onto the plastic door lock knob and was knocked unconscious. Mr. Richards was out of work for quite a while after the accident and then, not long after he was back home and working again, Mr. and Mrs. Richards separated and divorced. In the Ozzie and Harriet world of the 1950's, and especially in a small little community like the Highlands, this was a very, very big deal. Gary stayed with his dad—it was just the two of them—and Brooksie and I were never invited over again.

"It's gotta be a hundred and ten", Brooks said, puffing as we climbed the steepest part of the Hill.

"Or more," I said, "I'll bet it's even hotter than that."

Gary, who was bringing up the rear, said he guessed that it wasn't much over a hundred degrees but that it felt worse because of the humidity. We stopped for a rest under a big palm tree. We knew it was the only shade we'd see again until we hit the top.

"Gary, how do you know about the humidity?" I asked.

"We've got a barometer at home," he said matter-of-factly. "Actually, we've got seven barometers, although only three or four work." Gary was the second smartest kid in our class, after Brenda Bays. If anybody was going to know about humidity and what the temperature really was, it was going to be Gary Richards.

"Wow, seven barometers," Brooksie said. "I don't think we have even one at my house. Why you got so many, Gary?" Gary shrugged.

"Come on," I said, "let's keep going." It was early afternoon, and the sun was only going to get hotter. We trudged on.

Finally at the top of the Hill we stopped and took another breather. Gary's house was right at the top of the Hill….Brooks and I lived another mile or so, but the walking was much easier now that we'd made the top.

"Gary," Brooks said, "can I go in your house and use the bathroom? I gotta pee."

"No," Gary said, "I'm not allowed to have visitors….ah, when my dad's at work."

"I don't want to visit, Gary, I want to pee."

"Nope," he said, "no can do."

"Come on, Gary," I said, "give the guy a break. It's a half-hour walk home. If you don't want him to go in the house, just let him go in the back yard and piss."

"I told you, my dad said…."

"Your dad said not to bring anybody into your house for a visit. We're talking about whizzing in the backyard. Geez…."

Gary shrugged. "Okay," he grumbled, "but make it fast."

We waited for a break in traffic, went across the street and entered the backyard through a gate next to the garage. Once through the gate I stopped in my tracks and my mouth dropped open.

"Holy crap," I said.

"Holy double-crap," said Brooksie, "what is this stuff?"

"It's just my dad's stuff," Gary snapped, "my dad collects stuff."

"No kidding," I said, still taking it all in. The entire backyard was one huge pile of junk after another, dozens of piles, with just narrow walkways between them. Some piles were over six feet tall. Tires, car parts, cash registers, paint cans, (empty and full), piles of lumber, store displays, roofing material, stacks and stacks and stacks of newspapers and magazines…. unimaginable mountains of junk, organized, but just barely. Even under the patio covering leading into the house there were cardboard boxes stacked to the ceiling.

Gary looked over, read the amazement in my face and looked sheepish. "Hurry up, Brooks, take your piss," he said impatiently. Brooks had forgotten about peeing and was just wandering through the rows and rows of junk piled high.

Through the patio doors I could see into the house, and it was the same in there….piles and piles of newspapers and magazines and boxes and books, lots and lots of books. And trash: hamburger wrappers and paper coffee cups and donut boxes and shopping bags, mountains of shopping bags, all stacked neatly. It sure didn't look like this when I was here last, I thought to myself. That had been two years ago, before the accident and divorce.

I was standing next to a pile of electrical stuff—wires, old radios, tubes, switches—and a crude lean-to had been constructed over it in a half-hearted attempt to block the rain. There on the ground I spotted what first looked like a bent grey pipe about three inches in diameter and eight or ten feet long. But on further inspection I saw that it was a cable….inside the grey plastic skin were hundreds and hundreds of narrow, insolated strands of wire, wrapped together in pairs of two. I picked up one end.

"Gary, what's this thing? What's this used for?"

"It's not 'used' for anything," he said with an annoyed tone. "None of this stuff is 'used' for anything. It's just stuff my dad brings home. Okay, Brooks is finished. Now take off, guys, or I'm gonna get in trouble."

Brooksie and I left through the side gate and once we were on the sidewalk and well away from Gary's house, Brooks squealed, "Holy crapola! Did you see all that stuff?"

"See it? We were SURROUNDED by it. Like it was the 'Blob', but junk instead of a slime man."

"Yeah, the Blob! Man," Brooksie said, "how lucky is that guy to be living with all that cool junk?"

"I dunno, it didn't seem to me like Gary's feeling all that lucky with all that stuff stacked up."

It cooled off very little by the time I went to bed that night and even with the fan on I couldn't fall asleep. My mind was running on two parallel tracks. I was thinking about Gary Richards and about how things had changed for him and I was wondering why his dad would do that….collect all that junk, even in the house. But at the same time my mind was turning over and over the mental picture of that three-inch thick cable I'd seen on the ground in Gary's back yard. I estimated it had been a good ten feet, and there must have been 500 separate wires bundled together, each one with its own insulation. Ten times five hundred, divided by two (one positive and one negative) equaled twenty-five hundred feet. But what if it was twelve feet…. fifteen feet? What if there were only three hundred wires? Six hundred? I fell asleep doing the math, and at the same time thinking about my friend Gary and his crazy father and how much their life had changed.

Early the next morning Brooks and I were outside my bedroom window with a thirty-foot tape measure borrowed from my father's tool shed. About 25 feet from my window to the fence bordering our back yard with Mr. Laravee's back yard next door. Left turn and another 40 feet to the back of our property line. Right turn and just under 300 feet across the Laravee's back fence. Another right turn up the fence separating the Laravee and the Judd yards, about 40 feet. A final left turn and 20 feet from the fence to Brooksie's bedroom window.

"Four hundred and twenty-five feet!", I yipped. "We've got it, man. We can do this. Even if there's only a hundred pieces, and even if the cable's only ten feet, we got line to spare."

Brooks was less enthusiastic. "No," he said, "we do not 'got it'. Gary and his father have got it, and they have no reason to want to give it to us. We've got nothing, unless you want to count your retarded idea, which, by the way, I'm not buying."

(A quick word here. Yes, this is how we two twelve year-olds spoke. We'd been put into the same play pen as infants; as we learned to talk we'd created more or less our own language; by the second grade we were both going to 'speech' class three days per week; by the time we finally learned to talk like regular people, we both had an uncommon appreciation for language; and twenty or so years later, we both earned degrees in English. We grew up loving words and writing and language.)

"Who said anything about giving," I asked? "We're going to trade them for the cable. We'll find something just as good and swap."

"And if Mr. Richards doesn't want to swap?"

"You heard Gary yesterday. He said his dad brings stuff home and never looks at it again. Just lies there on the ground. What difference to Mr. Richards is it if a piece of cable's lying on the ground or, ah, say a radiator? We'll just make a trade, you know, kind of unanimously."

"You mean anonymously."

"That's what I said."

"Then you mean steal it."

"No, I don't mean steal it. I mean trade for it. And we'll find something really, really good, or we won't do it."

" I dunno," Brooksie said.

"Look, you'll be the judge, not me. If we don't find something that you agree is worth trading for the cable, then we won't do it."

Brooks looked unsure. He took his dark-rimmed glasses off and rubbed one eye, then the other. Too many times I'd talked him into schemes that had a way of going horribly wrong. (In fact, it's a dynamic that goes on to this day. Just last year we ended up lost and floating with the current on the backwaters of the San Joaquin Delta in a rented houseboat. But that's another story.) Finally he spoke.

"And you're sure you know how to make this thing work? You know how to do it that far? Four hundred and fifty feet?"

"Four hundred and twenty-five feet to be precise. And yes, I can make it work. WE can make it work. And it will be sooo boss. Whaddaya say?"

Brooksie put his glasses back on warily. "Well, okay, but it's got to be a trade."

We were, of course, talking about our very own telephone line from his house to my house. I was crazy for telephones and batteries and radios and speakers and such when I was a kid, and I'd figured out how to make them work….in a rudimentary sort of way. What could be more cool than two twelve year old best friends having their own, private telephone system?

It turned out that finding the items for the swap was the simplest part of the scheme. Walking home from playing baseball at Highland School, we passed a construction site and there, thrown on top of a garbage heap, was a complete, intact, though quite old and beat up looking, circuit panel, with breakers, a lid that closed, the whole deal. It had been torn out of the house that was being remodeled.

"I gotta admit," Brooks said, "this looks way, way more valuable than that old cable."

"Told you."

That night we did a "sleep out"….we would set up a pup tent in my back yard, Brook's back yard or in the canyon behind our houses, take our sleeping bags, some snacks and, presto, we were camping out under the stars. We'd been doing sleep outs ever since we were eight, so our parents never thought twice about it. That night we waited till about 2:00 a.m. and then, grabbing my dad's wheelbarrow, we headed to the construction site where we loaded up the discarded panel. It was a long walk to Gary's house, but the night was beautiful and warm and the moon was full and we were on another adventure. We took turns pushing the wheel barrow, ever mindful of the possible drive-by of a sheriff's cruiser;

as we walked we made up a laundry list of optional stories we could tell if one did drive by.

Once in the Richards' back yard, we were quiet as Indians. I pulled the cable out of the junk heap and then, ever so carefully, we lifted the circuit panel off the wheelbarrow on onto the ground, sort of tucking it in exactly where the cable had been. A quick, clean and quiet transaction. And I felt a very fair one. We lingered just a moment. The full moon illuminated the piles and piles of junk. I thought of Gary and the look I'd seen in his eyes that afternoon when Brooksie and I had stumbled onto his dad's "collection". Even as a twelve year old, I could sense his hurting. What did it mean?

From that night on, the summer passed quickly. We set up our little production room in the basement of my house and spent pretty much every waking hour splicing wire. Once we got it we found that the cable was much shorter than I'd estimated, just 72 inches, but there were 820 separate pieces of insulated wire inside, more than enough—eight times more—than we needed to span the 425 feet from Brooksie's bedroom window to mine. In all, we spliced together two sets of 75 wires (one positive, the other negative)—each splice required peeling off the insulation from two wire ends, twisting and crimping the two together, wrapping each joint with electrician's tape, and then doing a second wrap on the pair of joints. A lot of work for two kids, but we were passionate about the project, like two twelve year-old Alexander Graham Bells. (And of course the fact that there was a little larceny involved didn't hurt.)

My parents were curious about all the activity in the basement, particularly about where we'd acquired nearly five thousand feet of insulated wire. And we were totally, completely honest. We traded for it, traded an old, discarded fuse box for the old, discarded six-foot cable. Just junk, really…..junk for junk. Traded with who? Just some guy.

It took nearly two weeks to complete the splicing, and another couple days to carefully lay line along four hundred and twenty-five feet of fencing, test for breaks and fix each one we found. But finally the privately owned, Ricky-to-Brooksie telephone system was completed. I hooked up our two WW II army surplus handsets and a brand new 9-volt battery and…..YES! IT WORKED!….we were speaking to each other from our respective bedrooms. To us it was like connecting the eastern and western railroads, clicking out the first message on the Trans Atlantic cable, putting the first man in orbit. One giant step for Kid-Kind.

I saw Gary Richards only a few times the rest of the summer, once at the Plunge, another time at the grocery store where he and his father were shopping. Neither time was there anything to even remotely suggest that they were onto the unilateral trade I'd orchestrated. Every now and then I would find myself thinking about Gary and his dad and the junk in their yard and in their house. My instincts told me there was something wrong there, something not normal. But it wasn't my business, and there was nothing to do about it anyway.

Mainly Brooks and I spent the remainder of our summer vacation from school enjoying our new telephone line. We would bring friends over and do demonstrations. We would use the line to send

Morse Code, though the messages amounted mostly to SOS's. I hooked up my little 45 record player at my end of the line and a speaker at Brooksie's end and I was a DJ. And of course each night we would lie in our respective beds and whisper to one another under the covers....we had everything two twelve year-old best friends had to talk about, and that was a whole lot.

It was late one night near the end of summer that our private telephone line came full circle back to Gary Richards and his father. Brooks and I had been talking, probably about the Giants pennant run, about Mays and McCovey, when he announced he had to go pee. While lying there, waiting for my friend to return, with the handset to my ear, I heard voices in the receiver. This was nothing new....early on we'd discovered that the long telephone line, which was covered with the thinnest of insulation, would, on certain nights, act as an antennae, and pull in one of the more powerful radio stations broadcasting in the Bay Area. But this night was different in that the signal was quite strong and it was possible to make out every word in the broadcast. It was a talk show, KGO, and as I lay there waiting for Brooksie to return and absently listening, a string of words in the receiver suddenly caught my attention.

"So Don, when did this all begin? Can you remember when this hoarding compulsion began? When you first started bringing junk home?"

I sat up in bed.

"Oh, yes, I remember like it was yesterday. I was driving to work one morning in 1954. I worked as an analyst for the Department of Defense, and I was driving down the Virginia Turnpike on my way to the Pentagon. The north and southbound lanes of the Turnpike are separated by a broad, manicured lawn, and as I drove along, I noticed a magazine that had been thrown out onto the median. I didn't think anything about it, but on the way home that afternoon I saw that it was still there and I pulled over and picked up the magazine. Just like that. Didn't even think about why I wanted it….or that what I was doing was a little out of the ordinary. That's how it all started. This was the beginning of the unraveling of my life. I lost my job, my home, my family….. pretty much everything. And it all started with that magazine on the median strip."

"And you'd never exhibited any OCD hoarding behavior prior to that afternoon."

"No, Bob, I hadn't."

"I'd like to add something here if I may," a third voice said.

"Of course, doctor. Let me introduce to our listeners our second guest, Dr. Harold Freggiaro, nationally-known researcher at the Stanford School of Neurology. Welcome, doctor."

"Thanks, Bob. What I wanted to share is that Mr. Reynolds' experience is by no means typical. The vast majority of HOCD sufferers are born with the neural chemistry but the characteristic behaviors develop over quite a long time. They develop over quite a long time and usually aren't fully manifested until adulthood. Mr. Reynolds, on the other hand, was not "hard-wired" for HOCD from birth. Rather, it was a head injury sustained when he fell off a ladder in 1954, that…."

"Okay, I'm back. You there?"

"Shhhhh….quiet….listen Brooks.

"Huh? Listen to wh……"

"LISTEN!"

"…….sudden behavior caused by extraordinary pressure to a stunningly precise location on his head."

"Stunningly precise location, Dr. Freggiaro?" asked the announcer.

"Yes. You see each of us has a small collection of synapses, just above the temple, that controls our instinct to gather and store."

"Wait, you said 'gather and store'?

"That's right, Bob. Although critical to survival 80,000 years ago, the gather and store instinct is far, far less important to modern man, and hence this small center of brain cells is, for most of us, dormant and completely inactive. Only when a neuro-chemical imbalance exists at birth or, in the case of Mr. Reynolds, an injury to the head occurs at exactly the right spot, is the gather and store mechanism triggered."

"But, doctor, if it can be turned on, can it be turned off?"

"Not in the former case—cases where the brain chemistry is present at birth. But in some instances of head injury-related HOCD, yes. In the case of Mr. Reynolds, yes. In his case we were able to….."

There was a sudden and loud static crackling in the receiver, the voice became faint, and then it was gone.

"What was that all about?" Brooksie asked into the phone.

"I'll tell you what it was about. Gary Richards' dad has that HO-whatever. He's just like the guy on the radio. You heard it, Brooks. That explains all the junk at their house…. probably even explains Gary's mother leaving."

"Wow," Brooksie said, "son of a gun……"

We talked in whispers on our private telephone line for probably two hours. That we had to do something with what we'd learned was never in question. As facile as I was at stretching the truth, at dreaming up schemes, I had by twelve years of age developed a moral compass, and it was telling me I had to do something to try to help Gary and his dad. But what?

We could just go to Mr. Richards and tell him about what we'd heard ….about HOCD, about Dr. Freggiaro and how he could be fixed. But there were at least two problems with that option—first, we weren't even supposed to know that Gary's father was a crazy junk addict, let alone get involved with it. From the way Gary had behaved that day at the beginning of the summer, it was clearly a family secret, and our friend would be in big trouble for spilling the beans. And second, if we told Mr. Richards how we'd heard the radio show, he'd know about our private telephone line and he might put two and two together….might discover the "trade" we'd engineered. Sure, we could tell him that we'd heard it on the radio, but what were two twelve year olds doing listening to a discussion of obsessive compulsive disorders on KGO-TALK 810 at one o'clock in the morning? No, pre-adolescent logic dictated a course of action that was far, far out of the mainstream. We would write a letter to Mr. Richards from Dr. Freggiaro, the famed neurologist. To my best friend Brooksie and me, this made perfect sense.

By 9:00 a.m. the next morning, we were at the Greyhound Bus Terminal in Hayward, and two hours later we were in downtown Palo Alto walking the long two miles to Stanford Hospital.

"You think they're even gonna let us in there?" Brooks asked for the twentieth time since we'd left Hayward.

"They'll let us in….it's a hospital. They gotta let people in. If anyone asks we'll say we're visiting my mother."

"And what's she in for? They're gonna wanna know that."

"Tonsils."

"Kids have tonsils. Not adults. Better say she's having a baby," Brooksie said.

"Okay then. A baby."

Not two steps into the huge marble entry of the hospital, we were stopped by the security guard stationed next to the entrance.

"Can I help you boys?" he asked.

"Yeah," I said, "we're here to see my mom."

"What department?"

"Ah, Neurology," I said.

"Yeah," Brooksie quickly added, "his mom's having a baby."

The guard looked us over. "Then you'd be wantin' to go to Maternity,"

"Well, no sir, we need Neurology. My mom's having complications."

The guard's expression instantly turned to one of concern and sympathy.

"Oh, I see. Get on the elevator over there. Go to the third floor and turn to the right. And good luck."

"You idiot," I said once we were alone in the elevator, "why'd you tell him my mother was having a baby? You nearly got us thrown out."

"Because that's what we decided to say. Isn't that what we decided to say?" I rolled my eyes, he rolled his back.

We went to the Department of Neurology at Stanford Hospital because I was pretty sure there would be some kind of a sign or listing of doctors that would give us the correct spelling of Freggiaro's name, along with any title he might have besides doctor. Instead, we hit the jackpot. There on the counter were several pamphlets and brochures—one had information on all the doctors in the Neurology Department, including Harold

Freggiaro, and there was even a triple-fold piece on the department's research into Obsessive Compulsive Disorders, and bingo, HOCD was there. Perfect. I grabbed two of each and we headed back toward the elevator.

"May I help you?" A woman in a nurse's uniform had suddenly appeared at the counter.

"No," Brooksie said, "we're headed for Maternity. His mom's having a baby." He looked at me defiantely.

The next morning we visited Mildred White, my aunt who lived just across the street. Mildred White had a Remington typewriter, a big, pretty new one, and she'd let me use it before because she knew I was responsible and because I was her favorite.

"So what are you two up to?" My aunt asked with a laugh. Brooksie's face instantly drained of color.

"Up to? Nothing. Just need to type a letter to a guy. It's pretty important. Could we, ah, be alone, Mildred White?" (Note that I took great care not to lie to my aunt, even as I was about to commit forgery and identity theft to make sure my crime of burglary wasn't discovered and still be able to do 'the right thing'. Oh the web we weave.)

"Sure," she said, "I'll be in the bedroom if you need me."

It took Brooks and I two hours to write the letter, and this is what the final draft said….

August 29, 1960

Dear Mr. Richards,

I am Harold Freggiaro, MD, Neurology, Board Certified. I am from the School of Medicine, Washington University of St. Louis, Department of Neurology, 1953. I am working in the Department of Neurology at Stanford Hospital at the University of Stanford in Stanford, California. I am famous for knowing about OCD and Hoarding, which is what I think you might have and which I think I might be able to help you get cured of.

Give me a call at 415-651-3323.

Yours sincerely,

Harold Freggiaro, MD, Neurology, Board Certified

P.S. In case I might forget about writing this letter, please remind me about your junk problem when you call.

We addressed the letter using the Remington, we typed the return address of Stanford Hospital on it and we inserted one of each of the two pamphlets we'd retrieved the day before. The next day we Greyhounded back to Palo Alto, hiked to the hospital and posted the letter in a U.S. Mail Box in the big marble lobby. On our way out, we saw the security guard who'd questioned us two days before.

"So how's your mom, son?"

"Oh, she's fine," Brooksie answered for me, "had a boy....mother and baby are doing just great."

Brooks and I never found out what happened with the letter, or Mr. Richards. Six months after we started seventh grade at the big junior high school downtown, Gary moved away. It was three or four years later that I saw him again, and it was the last time. We were at a high school basketball game…he went to the other school. When I asked him how he was he said great. His dad had remarried and he liked his new mom. He looked okay to me. I couldn't really tell if his father had been cured of junk or whether Gary had just gotten used to it.

New Year's Eve with Buck Owens' Bus Driver
January 2003

Generally, I've been lucky in love. I say generally because there have been some, well, lonely periods in my life. Brief but painful. One such was my freshman year in college. The fall and winter of 1966 was a desolate year. A drought of a year girls-wise. So, not-surprisingly, my life-long, self-imposed ban on blind dating was temporarily lifted when on December 30th, 1966, I received a call from a good friend at Fresno State.

"She's cute, she's funny, she's smart, she's….."

"How smart?" I cut him off. "If she's too smart, we got problems." Larry Phillips, with whom I'd maintained a long-distance friendship through junior high and high school, always knew exactly what to say. "She's smart enough to carry on a conversation, but not such an egghead that she's gonna want to talk calculus all evening. And the party's gonna be out-a-sight. Lots of people.

A live band. Beer aplenty. And besides, what are you going to do if you don't drive down here?" He had me there.

"Alright," I said, "I'll come, but I've got a bad feeling about this." And I did, but even a stranger in Fresno was better than sitting home alone New Year's Eve. And then, as an afterthought, "Hey, if this girl is so great, why's SHE interested in a blind date on New Year's Eve?"

"Just broke up with her boyfriend. He's an idiot. She hates him. Excellent rebound action here."

So I drove from Hayward to Fresno. Kelly was cute and she was smart, but no one would have described her as funny on New Year's Eve, 1966. In a word, Kelly was miserable. In the space of the forty-five minutes we spent at my friend's apartment before leaving for the party, she and Larry's date, Kathy, disappeared into the bathroom three times, and each time Kelly came out, I could see she'd been crying.

"Hey, buddy," said Larry during one of the girls' disappearances, "don't take this personally; she just broke up with her boyfriend. They were pretty serious. Engaged, actually." Information he hadn't shared on the phone the day before. I had a sinking feeling. But Kelly was good looking, and I had a date with a girl and it was New Year's Eve. We left for the party.

Larry Phillips had lived in the Fresno area his whole life. "You gotta have radar to live here in the winter," he said from the back seat, "fog can get pretty ugly." The fog wasn't ugly, it was claustrophobic. A blinding, frightening gray void. I'd never seen anything like it before. Leaning up with his chin on the back of the driver's seat, Larry virtually drove the car by dictating instructions.

"Okay, a little further to the stop sign. Yeah, yeah. Okay. Stop. Now turn right. Turn, turn, turn….okay, straighten out." This went on for about five miles. Larry and Kathy stealing kisses between driving instructions, poor Kelly crying softly in the dark next to me. Five miles in forty-five minutes.

But once at the party, the evening began to look better. There was a live band like Larry had promised and, after a couple beers, Kelly and I were actually talking. I made her laugh and the bad feeling I'd had was beginning to lift. We danced a fast one. Another. Then a slow dance. Kelly felt good pressed against me….it had been a while. Then, midway through the slow dance, a little tap on my shoulder, a slight turn of my head to the right, and then a brilliant white flash of light. Then darkness. When my eyes blink open and I look up from the floor, I see that Kelly and the fiancé are tongue kissing. The marriage, I'm thinking, is on.

There was really only one intelligent, though clearly not manly, thing to do, and that was to get the hell out of that house as quickly as possible. No protest to Kelly that she'd done me wrong. No retaliatory punch. No looking around for Larry and Kathy. My eye throbbing and my head still reeling, I just grabbed my coat, got in my car and drove away. Into the fog.

Three hours later, give or take a few minutes, it was like a miracle. There was Larry's apartment building. I couldn't see the number, but through the fog I recognized an old Dodge pickup parked out front and then I saw the torn screen door to his apartment. It had taken me from New Year's Eve, 1966 until well into 1967, but I'd managed to find my way the five miles in the fog. And yes, oh yes, the front door was unlocked. All I could think about was going to bed….I just wanted to sleep and make the evening go away. I went straight through the living room in the dark, bumping into furniture, and into the bedroom and flicked on the light. There, in the bed, lay an old man holding an immense shotgun with a long, black, double barrel, and it was pointed directly at my stomach.

"Sit down, boy", he drawled, "sit down on the floor right where ya are and keep yer hands where I can see 'em. And don't say nothin'." I couldn't have spoken if I'd wanted to. My heart raced. I held my arms up in the air and almost lost my balance as I sat down on the floor cross-legged.

The old man, who wore striped pajamas and had thin blotches of shoulder-length graying red hair on his otherwise bald head, balanced the gun's barrel between his knees, the index finger of one hand on the trigger, the other index finger dialing 911.

"Okay," he said, "pohleese is 'a comin'. Now you stand up, boy." As I stood, arms still in the air, the old man got out of bed and motioned me into the other room. He followed and flipped on the light. This was not, I instantly realized, Larry's apartment.

"There, sit down on that couch, and keep yer hands in sight. You understand?"

I nodded. We looked at one another….looked directly into one another's eyes….for a long moment.

"Boy, put them damned arms down, fold 'em on your lap. Yer makin' me tired just lookinin' at ya." I obeyed. The double-barreled shotgun was now pointed generally in my direction, not directly at my mid-section. Progress, I thought. But I was still shaking.

The old man stared at me a while longer in silence. "Ya ain't here to rob me, or to kill me, are you?" I shook my head no. "Done come in here by mistake, I reckon. That right?" I nodded. "What's a' matter, boy, cain't you talk?"

"Ah, you told me to, ah, keep quiet."

The old man laughed. "Okay," he said, "now I'm a' tellin' ya to explain yerself. What's you doin' walking into my home?"

I told the old balding man in striped pajamas my story, from arriving that afternoon in Fresno, to walking mistakenly into his apartment.

"Yup, he gotcha a good 'un. Eye's like to swell shut. You just sit there. Git up and I'll shoot ya," he said with a chuckle. The old man un-cocked the shotgun, leaned it against the wall, and disappeared into the little kitchenette. "Here," he said returning, "put this on yer eye." It was an enormous piece of round steak and it felt good and cold and soothing on my face.

"That be my New Year's dinner, so don't you be sneezin' on it. You hear?"

"I hear."

By now it was two a.m. "Want a pull of white?" the old man asked. "White?" I asked. He laughed.

The old man handed me a mason jar. "This'll make that eye feel even better."

And so there we sat, me on the old worn couch, him on an overstuffed 50's-style rocker, passing the jar back and forth, till the sun came up.

His name was Jimmy Butane (pronounced "Bo-tan") and he told me that he worked for Buck Owens. He drove Buck's bus when the band toured, did some mechanical work on it, and did pretty much nothing at all when the band wasn't touring. "They's down in Bakersfield tonight, at the Palace, doin' a big show," he said. "Ol' Buck he said I should go down there but, hell, a ol' man like me, what would I be 'a doin' at the Crystal Palace on New Year's Eve?" Jimmy told me stories of being on the road with Buck and the Buckaroos. At the time I barely knew who Owens was, but even so, Jimmy's stories were spellbinding. Jimmy had been there from the beginning of Buck's career….he knew everyone Buck knew, had been everywhere Buck had been. Oh, to be able to talk to him now, knowing what I know about the music.

When the sun came up and the fog started to burn away, Jimmy asked if I wanted to go to Denny's for breakfast. "They put on a nice breakfast there," he said.

"But what about the police?" I asked, just then remembering that he'd called 911 hours before. "Oh, hell," he said, "that damned phone don't even work. Aint' never worked. I jus' use it for burglars….and murderers. Like you, boy."

"But what if I'd actually been a robber or a killer?" I asked.

"Hell, boy, that's what my shotgun's fer." The old man laughed and we went to Denny's to ring in the New Year, 1967.

Just About Four Seconds Flat
April 1970

(Note: Just About Four Seconds Flat is a story I wrote while in graduate school. All of the other stories in this collection are mostly autobiographical; this one is clearly not. The reader is warned that both strong language and strong content is contained in the story that follows. RC)

Four rides in four hours, and only a hundred miles. I was pissed. Six miles outside of Turlock, with six hundred to go. Twelve noon on the hottest day of the year, and me without even a tree to stand under.

And then, outta' nowhere, this big old fancy blue van pulls over and stops, and the next thing I know I'm haulin' butt down 99.

"Where to?" the cat asks, and I say Mexico.

"Well then, you're in luck, son. I'm going down that way myself. We should make the border by sundown."

I nod my head but don't say no "thank you sirs". Little while later the cat looks over at me and says ain't it just a beautiful day for drivin' and I say, "Sure is," wondering how much the cat would like this here 'beautiful day' if he was stuck out there in that sun and didn't have no fancy-assed air-conditioner to keep him cool.

He didn't say no more after that, and in a while I got to feelin' pretty good about ridin' all the way to Mexico in his big old air-conditioned van. Only hassle now would be at the border.

We stopped for gas just south of Fresno. I jumped out of the van, stretched my legs and then walked across the street to buy a pack of smokes. It was a little trucker's café packed full of truck drivers, and when I ask for change, this old fat bitch of a waitress say's she ain't got no time to be making change. I tell her that's fine, if she ain't got the time, I'll just jump over the fuckin' counter and take care of it myself. It don't take more than four seconds flat for her to make my change, but when I come walkin' out of the joint with my cigarettes, I see that big old blue van is gone, and my suede jacket gone with it.

Right then and there I decide to kill the motherfucker if I ever lay eyes on him again, but before I can do anymore decidin', the cat taps me on the shoulder and says do I want a coke. So the next thing I know, I'm sittin' back in the truck stop, sippin' on an extra large root beer and thinkin' how glad I am I don't have to kill the motherfucker.

We got to talking in the cafe. He asked me how come I was goin' down to Mexico, like on a vacation, or what? So I say, sure, a vacation, and I tell the cat about how I got these rich friends down in Ensenada, and how these rich old friends of mine got themselves some villa rented right on the beach, and I go on and on, with him eatin' it all up. Then I ask him why he's goin', knowing damn well he ain't goin' for the same reason I am. Cat's too straight, and got too much money. 'Course I know plenty cats who got money and still go down to score. That's how they get it in the first place. Lots of money in that shit if you know who you're buyin' from. But he says he's going just to take some pictures and mess around, and I believe him 'cause he looks too straight to be doin' anything else.

I ask him what kinda' pictures, but before he can say anything, the fat old bitch of a waitress comes up to the table with our check. She gives me a badass look and I give her one right back.

"Well, we'd better head out if we're going to make it by sundown." He says this and then he pulls out his wallet and gives her a ten. I'd say 'bout the hardest thing I ever had to do in my whole life was to unglue my eyes from that dude's big fat wallet. Man, it was so full of bread the cat had to use both hands to stuff it back into his pocket. That's when I got me a plan.

Between Bakersfield and L.A. I did most of the talkin'. I was having a good old time tellin' this chump about how I was a college student, and how I got a football scholarship and was studyin' to be a scientist or a doctor, I couldn't decide which, and just going on and on with my fine line of crap. And he just drove and nodded his head, eatin' it all up, but not sayin' much. After a while, though, I got to runnin' out of things to tell him, so I asked him about the pictures he was gonna to take in Mexico. The guy told me that he was a teacher, which I already kind of figured, and that picture takin' was just his hobby. His 'avocation', he said.

"So, like, what kind a' pictures you take, man?"

"All kinds," he says. "Here, you can see for yourself. There's a book in the glove compartment with some of my photos."

I open up the glove box and reach inside for the book, but the first thing my hand hits is somethin' cold and smooth. And next to it there's a box of bullets—thirty-two's. I grab the book and close the glove box real quick. Son of a bitch, I think to myself, this is some sweet ride to Ensenada I got me.

It was a thick book with a plastic cover, like they have in libraries. I read the title—'Life-Loving: Photos and Verse by George Arents'. I turned it over and I'll be damned if the cat's picture wasn't on the back. There was a camera slung over his shoulder and he was standing next to his fancy blue van. "George Arents" it said, "educator, poet and one of the most exciting new photographers on the American scene, makes his home in…." I quit reading and looked at the cat.

"Hey man, this is you." He just smiled and kept his eyes on the road.

"Wow, like, you're famous, man. Says here you're a poet and everything."

"I'm not much of a poet, I'm afraid. Do you like poetry?"

"Man, I love poetry. I read all that shit in college."

'Course I lied about diggin' poetry just like I lied 'bout goin' to college. But I figured I'd read a couple of old George's poems and then tell him how triple-stone-outta sight they was. Well, I got to readin' and, funny thing is, them poems of his were okay. Really, they weren't no poems at all, they were just little stories with pictures to go with 'em. There was stories in the big old book about almost anything you could think of.

There was this one about how the cat gets up real early one mornin' figuring to go to the beach. But he sees it's raining and cloudy and shit outside, so he decides not to go after all. He just spends the day moping 'round the house, feelin' all bummed out. That's all there was to the story, 'cept that, near the end, he thinks maybe it would have been good to have gone after all, that maybe it would have been pretty at the beach just the same. And sure enough, you look across the page, and there's the ocean, just about the prettiest damned ocean you ever saw. And you figure that it was the rain that made it that way and that old George, he shoulda' gone.

'Course not all the stories was about him, only the ones with "I"'s and "we's". Some of 'em was about other folks. Like this one I read where these two little nigga kids is playin' on the sidewalk. The story told about how they'd just play and play on the fuckin' sidewalk, and about all the fun they was havin' just kickin' a Pepsi can back and forth. 'Cross from the story there was a picture of this big old mountain with trees and streams and green grass and everything. Way far away on top of the mountain you could see these two people ridin' on horses. Well, I looked a long time at that mountain tryin' to make sense out of it. It was about the best lookin' mountain I ever laid eyes on, but it sure as hell didn't fit with the story that was across the page. I read the story again, and saw that it was called the same thing as the book—Life-Loving.

"Say man, what's this here 'life-lovin'' mean? You got it in two different places. What's it mean?"

"It means anything you want it to mean," he says, without taking his eyes off the road. But I could see he was smilin'.

"Shit, man, I don't WANT it to mean anything. You the cat wrote it, ain't you?"

"Sure I wrote it," George said, "But you're reading it." He was grinning at me like I was some kinda damned fool.

"Just 'caus I don't understand your motherfuckin' poooettttreeee don't mean you got to laugh at me." I was pissed and he could see it, 'cause he quit grinning and looked over at me all serious-like.

"I was NOT making fun of you," the asshole said. "I was only laughing because the question you asked, many other people have asked, and I've never been able to give a good answer." Now it was my turn to laugh.

"You sayin' you wrote this here story 'bout some niggas playin' on the sidewalk, and you don't even know what it means?"

"No, I mean that I don't know how to…." He stopped and looked over at me again. He had a funny kind of look, like he had a pain somewhere that he couldn't do nothin' about.

"Alright," he said, "I'll tell you what life-loving means. You like that picture there?" He pointed at the green mountain with the horses and stuff and I nodded.

"So you like the photo?" he asked.

"It's okay I guess."

"What's okay about it?"

I thought for a second. "I like the trees. And I like them horses."

"You like the trees because they're green and beautiful and lovely?"

I looked at the cat thinkin' maybe he was puttin' me on, but his face said he wasn't so I answered him.

"Yeah, George," I said, they're fine lookin' trees. But what's that got to do with this life-lovin' jive?"

"Life-loving is just a way to describe in words the way those trees make you feel. It means that they're alive and you're alive and you love them because they're beautiful. It means they bring you pleasure, and that makes you love life. That's all."

"But what about this story here that goes with the picture? The one about the kids. They sure as hell don't think that old dirty sidewalk of theirs is luv-ell-lee." I said this real nasty, figurin' I had him there.

"But maybe they DO think the sidewalk is beautiful, or perhaps it gives them some pleasure. Don't you understand, it DOES give them something? They can play kick-the-can on it....they can play hop-scotch, they can...."

"No chance, man. When I was a kid, I had me the same old sidewalk in the baddest hood in East Oakland there is. Only pleasure that sidewalk ever gave me was when my old man used to give me a quarter for cleaning up the mess the whores and their johns used to make in front of our house ."

"And when you got your quarter, what did you do with it? Did it make you happy or sad?"

"I ain't NEVER been sad 'bout getting' me some money, dude, that is for damn sure. But no sidewalk ever give me money, no sidewalk ever give me nothing."

Old George he didn't say nothin' for a long while after that. He just kinda' stared out at the road with that look of his. I was just about to tell him that I didn't give a damn about his poetry crap anyhow when he spoke.

"It's like this," he starts out slow, "those kids in the poem have the same amount of potential for......ah, they have the same amount of love in them that you or I or the people in that picture have. If they lived on that mountain, they would see its beauty and they would love it. But they don't live on the mountain, they live in the city, and so they find beauty and a reason for loving life there, where they live. You see, beauty is a relative value that...."

"You ever live in East Oakland, man? Ever even BEEN THERE? Ain't a whole lot to love 'round there 'cept a little ass when you can get it."

"No, I've never lived in Oakland, but I know…."

"Man, you don't know shit then." We didn't talk no more after that.

I slept for a long while, and when I woke up we was already through L.A. Old George, he had the radio goin', listenin' to some crazy-ass baseball game. I don't care nothin' 'bout baseball so I got to lookin' through that book again. This one story was about this dude n' chick ballin' and just makin' fine damn love. I didn't get the way it ended, but I didn't ask no more questions. There was a lot more good stories to read, with good pictures too, so I'd just skip over the bullshit parts that didn't make no sense.

I must a' gone through half that book before I noticed my first dog race sign. You can always tell when you're getting close to T.J. 'cause of all the dog race signs.

"How much further?" That was the first thing either of us had said since before the Grapevine. I figured the cat was still pissed at me for sayin' what I said. And I didn't fuckin' care.

"Only a few more miles," he said, without looking from the road.

I got to thinkin' about crossin' the border. There was a chance they wouldn't let me through. They pulled that on me once before. 'An undesirable' is what I was. Fuckers. Took me nearly a day to sneak through, and by the time I got to the Ensenada people who I was s'posed to drive for, they'd found somebody else. Always cats around waitin' to drive shit across the border. I gave myself an extra day this trip, but I was still plenty nervous about makin' it on time.

It was after six when we got to the border. The place was jammed with cars and we had to wait about twenty minutes before they signaled us to pull up. When we were half way through the island, two fat Mexicans in uniforms came up to the van, one on each side. The one on my side stuck his head through the window and checked out the back, but not before he gave me the once over. "What's this n_____ doin' in this fancy assed van", I could hear him thinkin'.

"Vacation" was all George said. The Mexican on his side nodded and asked, "How long?" The other guy was still looking the back of the van and me over.

"Oh, I'd say about a week. Going just south of Ensenada."

Now both the Mexicans was lookin' at me.

"What about him?" one of them asked George pointing at me. "Maybe you better get out of the van and…."

"Now, wait a minute. This young man is traveling with me. He's one of my students. We drove down to try our luck at deep-sea fishing. Is that a crime?"

"That's right, officer, sir, we gonna do some of that deep sea fishin'. Hey, they bitin'?"

The two Mexicans waved us through.

We drove straight through Tijuana without stoppin' or sayin' a word. I think the old dude was a little nervous about lyin' and he just wanted to get back on the open road. In twenty minutes we were driving along the coast with T.J. behind us.

"Hey man, thanks." I said it without looking over at him.

"Not a problem," was all he said.

I got to thinkin 'bout how it was a pretty damn decent thing he done. How he could a' threw my ass right out of the truck, especially after what I said about him and his book.

"You know," I said after a while, "I been thinkin'. I guess some folks might think a sidewalk was a good thing. I mean, if that's all they had was a sidewalk." George looked over at me and smiled. He didn't say nothin', but I knew that patched things up.

We were about thirty minutes from Ensenada when I got to thinkin' about the plan.

"Pay road's just up ahead. You always take the pay road, man?"

"It's fastest, isn't it?"

"Maybe, but those fuckin' Mexican bandits want too much money, they'll soak ya every chance they get. Best way's the old mountain road, don't cost a cent."

"That's alright," George said, "it won't break me."

No shit, I thought.

"Well, I'll tell ya' why I like the old mountain road. It's the view, man, the fuckin' view. Christ, you can see half 'a Mexico from up there. Bet you could get some good pictures from up there. And ya know, I was thinkin', the toll cops could end up hasslin' me like those two fat fucks back at the border."

"All right," he says suddenly, "the old mountain road it is. Where's the turn off?" And just like that, the plan comes together.

In half an hour we hit the summit. It was just a few more miles into Ensenada and we hadn't seen a car since we'd turned off the highway. The mountain road was so bad even the Mexicans didn't use it much. I was countin' on that.

I waited until I saw a place for old George to pull over, and then I sat up in my seat and looked at him like my eyes were gonna' bug right outta my head.

"Wow", I said, "just look at that damn fine sunset. If that ain't a life-lovin' sunset I ain't never seen one. Make a good picture for one of your books.

"You think so?"

"I KNOW so, man, that there's one lovely old sunset." From the summit the pay road looked like a little piece of string winding along the beach, and beyond that you could see the sun easing down all red and yellow into the ocean.

"Maybe you're right", he said. Old George slowed the van down and parked right in the place I'd picked out for him. Then he grabbed his picture takin' shit and walked over to the ledge. I got out too and stretched my legs. The old dude looked excited and he was hurryin' with his little three-legged camera stand so as not to miss the sun before it went down. I walked over to where he was standin' and looked over the edge.

"One helluva long ways down."

George was still fiddling with his camera and he didn't even hear me. I went back to the van and got in. The keys were still in the ignition. I watched as he fooled with the camera.

"Come here," George shouted over his shoulder, "I want to see what you think of this shot before I snap it."

"Okay", I yelled, reaching into the glove compartment. My hands were shaking a little, but I took three bullets out of the box and loaded them into George's pistol. I stuck the gun in the pocket of my suede coat and walked over to him.

"Take a look through the shutter." He had a grin on his face a mile wide. Man, did this cat have a pretty sunset to shoot. I bent over the three-legged stand and put my eye up to the little peephole.

"Prettiest damn sunset I ever seen, dude." I stepped back. "Better go for it though, 'fore the sun goes down any further."

He stepped in front of me, and when he bent over the camera I took the pistol out of my pocket and emptied it into his head, right above the left ear. George fell over sideways and his arm hooked on the three-legged stand and they both went down. I ran over to the van and started it up, then drove it right to the edge of the cliff, jumped out and loaded George into the back, making sure not to get any blood on my coat. I reached in his pocket and grabbed that big old fat wallet. Then I threw the camera and the stand into the front seat, the seat I'd been sitting in all day, and slammed the door shut. I figured it'd be worth some money, but I didn't like the idea of carryin' it all the way into town.

I went around to the other side of the van and reached in for the automatic gearshift. I was just about to pull it down into drive and step back when I remembered the book. I reached over and grabbed it out of the glove box, pulled the gearshift down and them jumped back.

That big old blue van made it down to the bottom in just about four seconds flat. From where I was standing old George's van looked like a crumpled up milk carton thrown on a garbage heap.

The sun was all the way down when I started walking, but it still lit part of the sky yellow and red and pink. One damned pretty sunset, I thought. And it got me to thinkin' about all them good stories in George's book, and about all them good pictures that went with 'em. That old George, I thought, that cat was really somethin'. One smart son of a bitch, 'cept when it came to that life-lovin' jive. Ain't nobody gonna' be lovin' life while they're playin' on some crappy old sidewalk.

Post Script

When I was twenty-one and enrolled in graduate school at San Jose State University I entered a short story called Just About Four Seconds Flat in a writing contest. The contest was called the Phalen Competition, which included student entrants from San Jose State, Santa Clara University and Stanford. There were various awards for poetry, blank verse, essays and short stories, but there was an overall prize for the very, very best entry of all, regardless of the category. And the overall prize was $500 (a HUGE amount of money for a college student on loans in the early seventies), but even better, the prize included being the guest of honor at a dinner hosted by novelist Kurt Vonnegut.

After Hemmingway, Vonnegut was, and still is, my favorite American novelist, and the thought of hearing him speak at a banquet, much less sitting next to him at dinner, chatting with the guy, just looking into his eyes, was, well, almost more than I can describe even all these years later. And yes, a week before the banquet, I received a letter in the mail informing me that Just About Four Seconds Flat had won two awards: best short fiction and OVERALL GRAND PRIZE. I couldn't believe it. I cried and danced around the apartment and my wife and friends and the whole neighborhood celebrated for two days. Lots of us in our little group were want-to-be writers and the award was, in a way, recognition for our entire little artist community.

I went out and bought a cheap sport coat and got a haircut and wrote and re-wrote and re-re-wrote my acceptance speech. And then I waited and waited for that Wednesday night when I'd meet Kurt Vonnegut and he'd say something like, 'kid, I liked your story' or 'pal, you may just have what it takes' or even just 'hey, not bad'. It really didn't matter what he would say, because I knew he'd be there, in San Jose that night, because of me. ME.

About mid morning on the big day the phone rang. It was a guy I knew from my Tuesday and Thursday morning writing class….

not really a friend, an acquaintance. "Hey, man, we missed you last night. What a bummer. Vonnegut was great. He even made a joke about you. Said you stood him up. Where were you, man?"

I got on my motorcycle and drove the 12 blocks to the English Department in Thompson Hall on Seventh Street. I wept all the way, the chilly wind drying the tears almost as quickly as they rolled across my cheeks but, even though I stopped in the men's room to wash my face, I knew that the secretary could see I'd been crying. She recognized me right off, knew, I'm certain, why I'd missed the dinner, and shook her head as if to say, 'there, there.' She handed me an enveloped. "You'd better check inside just to make sure," she said softly. Yes, there was one check for $200 and another one for $500.

It would be over thirty years before I wrote another short story. Kurt Vonnegut died a few years back. I know this is goofy, but I've sort of half believed, all these years since 1971, that someday, somehow, I'd get to meet that guy. And in my imagining he'd remember 'Just About Four Seconds Flat' and he'd say, 'You know, pal, you shoulda stuck with it. You shoulda.'

Broken Crown
September 2008

There was a lot to admire about my mother. I think what I admired, and to be honest, envied, most about her was the absoluteness and utter resolve with which she held to her priorities in life. I suppose part of that was simply a matter of her generation's need to keep its eye on the prize if it was going to survive a devastating economic depression and then a horrific world war. But even among her contemporaries, let's say among her seven sisters and three brothers with whom she'd huddled in a sod shack in the Dakotas during the dusty time, Millie stood out as a person who kept sight of what was most important…..in her case, her family, and every fiber of her four-foot-eleven frame was laser focused on keeping and protecting it. Growing up I can recall many stories that cast a light on this preoccupation of my mother's, but few more dramatically than the time she went after the guy who broke my crown.

I can tell you the exact year. It was 1965, the year 'Batman the Movie' came out. This was the first one, with the TV series cast, Adam West and Burt Ward, and the crazy camera angles and the WHAM, SPLAT, BOF cartoon graphics punctuating the fight scene punches. I was a junior in high school and, as such, I normally didn't get in a lot of actual movie watching in at the drive-ins, (if you catch my drift), but this night I was with Stevie, (derived from Stephanie), and she and I were just marginally interested in one another romantically. She was a very funny girl from another high school and we made one another laugh, especially when supplied with a non-stop stream of material from the caped crusaders.

After the movie I took Stevie straight home and we parked in her parent's driveway; they were well-off and lived in the country on a couple acres of land. We'd be left alone, and laugh time was over. I remember I'd set the brake on my '56 VW bug and I was just leaning over and reaching my right arm around Stevie when suddenly my body was wrenched back with the force of a 'jaws-of-life' claw and what felt like a steel pipe was shoved into my mouth. It went in deep, scraping the roof of my mouth and digging into the soft skin in the back of my throat. I was trying to see what was happening, who was doing this to me, but it was dark. Then Stevie started screaming.

"Lance, Lance, stop! STOP! STOP!" She was hysterical, screaming at the top of her lungs.

"Yeah," came a bellowing response, "I'll stop. I'll stop after I kill this piece of (expletive)."

And in a terrifying flash I knew exactly what and who. The WHO was Stevie's ex-boyfriend and the WHAT was the barrel of a pistol shoved in my mouth. My eyes were squinted shut, I was holding my breath and my heart pounded in my chest a base drum from my high school's marching band, only faster. I distinctly remember wondering if my last night on earth was going to be distinguished by having watched what was probably the worst movie of the 1960's. WHAM, SPLAT. Funny what pops into your head when you think you're going to have your brains blown out of your skull by a jealous boyfriend.

And then, as quickly as it had happened, it was over. Lance, the crazed, apparently not-so-ex, junior college football playing, boyfriend jerked the steel barrel out of my mouth, cracking the crown in my lower left quad in the process, and then ran up the driveway laughing and screaming like a wild Indian who'd just scalped a white settler. As Lance got into an awaiting car I heard the sound of more laughter….a carload of Indians.

Stevie was sobbing. "Are you okay?" she kept asking. "Are you okay? I'm so sorry. So, so sorry. Are you okay? Are you okay?" I said I was, even as I spit blood and the awful taste of metal out on the concrete driveway. We sat for a minute in the darkness and Stevie's sobbing melted to sniffles. Finally….

"What are you going to do?"

"What do you mean," I asked.

"You know, like, are you gonna go looking for Lance? What a loser he is. Cause if you are, I wanna come along." I detected a hint of excitement in her voice. Then she leaned over and kissed me on the lips.

Stevie and I went to different high schools, we lived in different towns, hung out with different groups of friends and, as I was quickly deducing, had very, very different reactions to near-death experiences.

"No," I said, "I'm going to go home. Right now. My mouth hurts."

It was a forty-minute drive from Fremont back to Hayward and I don't think it's at all an exaggeration to say that my mind covered more ground in that forty minutes than during any forty day period of my short, seventeen-year life. As I sped by the illuminated billboards that lined Highway 17, I thought back trying to remember any other times in my life when I'd come close to dying, or at least thought I'd come close. There was the time when I was barely out of infancy and my father held me by the back of my pajamas, dangling me out of a second story window as a practical joke on my old uncle Louie (nearly killed him); the time my cousin Tommy pushed me off a dam into rushing water, (nearly killed me); the time Tommy, (same sadist cousin), shot me in the ear with a BB gun, (he was aiming for my eye); and the time my buddy Chuck and I rolled his De Soto on Crow Canyon Road (we just left the car there and walked home…..idiot kids). Driving down 17 that night in the dark in my little black VW, none of these incidents seemed even in the same league as the gun in the mouth. If the big jealous linebacker boyfriend had pulled the trigger he'd have put a hole through the back of my throat, right where my spinal cord attached to my brain. Man, would I be dead. With this thought I realized that I was shaking and my teeth were actually chattering, I mean audibly clicking together. Obviously it was some sort of delayed reaction; I was more terrified driving home than I'd been in Stevie's driveway.

Even before I could step through the front door my mother was there, grasping my left forearm, squeezing it like a vice as she pulled me across the threshold.

"What's wrong? What happened?"

"Huh? What? Whaddahya mean? Nothing's wrong."

I tried to pull away but she wouldn't release my arm.

"Now you listen here, I want to know what happened tonight, and I want to know right now. And why is there blood on your mouth? Were you in a fight?"

"No, I was not in a fight. I do not fight. You know that. Now let me come in and we'll sit down and I'll tell you about a very crazy experience I had tonight."

Millie had a unique and supernatural gift—she knew things about her children, my sister and I, before she could possibly know them. Sometimes even before they happened. My mother wasn't a clairvoyant in the general sense….her gift of knowledge was very specialized, very focused on her kids. She just knew things.

(Here's a fairly typical example—some years after the broken crown incident, I was working as a free lance writer and, without much warning, was sent back to New York City to do some research. As luck would have it, the dad of a friend of mine had an old beat up car in Manhattan that he needed driven back to Palo Alto and I offered to fairy it home figuring it would save me air fair. On the way home, I stopped over in Cleveland to get some sleep and from my motel room I called my wife. No answer. It was a Sunday night so I guessed she was visiting her parents in Hayward. Nope, not there. So I tried my parents home thinking she might have stopped off there. My mother answered...."Oh, Ricky, Ricky, I'm so glad you called. I've been worried sick about you all day. Last night I dreamt you were in a terrible car accident. You were driving in the Rocky Mountains in a little white car and you tumbled off the road and down a mountain side and you were just lying there and calling out but no one was there to help." So, here's the deal. My mother didn't know I was driving across the country, actually headed toward the Rockies, (she thought I was calling from home in San Jose) and she certainly wasn't aware I was driving a little white Toyota sedan. I should add that from the next day forward I've always worn a seat belt.)

We sat down at the kitchen table and both of us lit cigarettes. (Yes, in 1965 mothers and sons smoked together.....I know, it seems strange now even to me.) For a moment I considered lying about what happened. If my mother's gift was focused clairvoyance, mine was deft story telling; I'd had seventeen years of practice lying to my mother and there was no one better at fabricating on his feet. But I thought better of it. Why not tell her the truth? It would sure be easier than lying and besides, it might make me feel better.....calm me down, maybe.

So I told my mother the story of the jealous boyfriend who shoved a pistol in my mouth and threatened to kill me. I only changed one part—I told her that afterward, when Lance left with his friends, I found the pistol on the driveway and found it was a toy....a cap gun. She listened to the entire story in silence and then got up, walked into the laundry room and returned with a flashlight.

"Open your mouth," she said. I obliged and Millie shined the flashlight in my mouth. Then she stuck her index finger in and felt around.

"OUCH", I yelped, "that hurts."

"Hurts? HURTS? I'll tell you what hurts. Do you know that your father and I haven't even paid for that crown yet? Now, tell me, and tell me this minute. Who did this to you? Who is this joker with the cap gun?" She took hold of my chin with her thumb and index finger and squeezed hard. My mother's deep blue eyes burned. "I want his name, NOW! He's going to pay to have that crown fixed. So help me!"

Naturally I lied and told my mother I didn't know the joker's name. First and foremost, there was a good chance this Lance idiot was dangerous, and I sure didn't want my mother coming into contact with him. (I say 'chance' because, in truth, I honestly did feel that it WAS possible the gun was a toy and that the jerk was just trying to scare me.) Second, having your mother go after your enemy is just about the most humiliating turn of events that could happen during one's high school career, right after cheating on your girlfriend and having her find out from her sister during Sunday dinner after which she, the girlfriend, throws a crystal salt shaker across the dining table, family looking on in horror, and her, the sister, breaking her nose two days before the big Home Coming game at which she, the sister, presides as head cheerleader, or would have if not for the broken nose thing. But that's another story. And lastly, I lied because I just wanted the whole thing to go away. (Fat chance with Millie on the case.)

But to my surprise, my mother, who could be as tenacious as a dog with a bone, released my chin and kissed me on the forehead. "You go to bed," she said, "you look tired."

"What are you going to do?" I asked suspiciously.

"Me, I'm going to bed."

"You know what I mean, about this crown thing."

Millie gave me another peck on the forehead. "Don't you worry," she said, and left the kitchen.

The stress of the gun-in-the-mouth adventure the night before must have knocked me for a loop because it was nearly eleven a.m. the next morning when I awoke to the sound of the phone ringing.

"Hello," I answered, still more asleep than awake.

"Oh my God. Oh my God, Rick. Oh my God."

"STEVIE?" I felt adrenaline wash through my body.

"Oh my God. Your mother."

"What about my mother? Stevie, what about my mother?"

"She was just here. At my house."

"Your house, that's crazy. She doesn't even know where you live."

"Well, you're sure wrong about that, because she was just here and I'm in HUGE, HUGE trouble and I'm grounded for life and I'm freaking out here. Why did you tell your mother? You are such a loser"

"Tell her what?" A stupid question, I admit, but I was panicking.

"About Lance, you LOSER! About Lance and his gun!" She was crying now and I could hear her mother screaming in the background.

"Stevie, slow down. My mother was at your house? Why?"

"To find out where Lance lives. Oh, and to tell my mother about what happened last night so that my life could be ruined," she sobbed.

"You didn't tell. TELL ME YOU DIDN'T TELL HER WHERE HE LIVES. YOU DIDN'T, RIGHT?"

"I tried not to, but she wouldn't let up. Your mother is brutal. Do you know that? BRUTAL! And then my mother jumped in. It was horrible. It's like, they were making each other crazy, like they were feeding off each other. Why in God's name did you tell your mother about Lance and the gun?"

"I, ah, I told her it was a toy gun. She believed me."

"TOY GUN? Are you kidding me? LANCE MC LUAGHLIN WITH A TOY GUN? You idiot, that was his brother's 9 mm Glock. I've shot that thing before."

"It was real? Really?" There was a long silence and then a sigh on the other end.

"Look, I've got to get off. Don't ever call me again."

"Wait, Stevie, wait. Where does Lance live? Is my mother going there?"

"Oh, she's going there alright, and God help Lance if he's home. Don't call me you loser! Lossss-errrrr"

"Wait Stevie. Where does Lance live?"

"In Union City. East Doering. Meadow Apartments. Number 28. LOSER!" Then Stevie hung up.

East Doering was just two exits before Stevie's exit. The night before I'd driven that distance in thirty minutes. That Saturday morning it was more like fifteen. I'd already decided that if a CHP red-lighted me I'd just keep on going right to Lance's apartment. My little bug was whining like I had a whip to it. The adrenaline I'd felt the night before was nothing like I felt now. I just kept thinking of my mother, her tiny four foot eleven inch frame, standing at #28, pounding on the door till someone answered. And it was all my fault. Stevie was right, why did I tell her about the gun? What was I thinking? And what was I going to do when I got there? As I'd run out of the house I'd unconsciously grabbed an aluminum baseball bat in the garage. What in God's name was I going to do with a baseball bat? I'd never hit anyone with the intent to hurt them in my entire life, let alone bludgeoned anyone with a blunt object. And how would an aluminum baseball bat stand up against a 9mm Glock? Truth is, I didn't know what I was going to do when I got to Lance's apartment, I just knew I had to get there fast.

East Doering was a country road that bounded the little town of Union City on its north end, with scattered development, including some run-down apartments on one side of the street and hay fields and cattle on the other side. As soon as I was off the freeway I spotted the Meadow Apartments, a dingy, dark grey two-story cinder block structure that looked all the world like a state penitentiary. All the apartments faced the street and I slowed down till I spotted #28, slammed on the breaks, jumped out of the car and ran up the stairs. The door was open and I rushed in.

"Hey Dude, sorry about your tooth." Lance was sitting on a ratty floral couch. It was ripped and stained. One of his roommates sat next to him on the couch, a second on an aluminum lawn chair. All three were wearing only boxer shorts, except Lance who also wore a pair of white tube socks. They sat with their feet up on a giant cable spool coffee table, circa 1965, and passed around a massive glass bong. Half of the 1965 Chabot Junior College offensive line. One of the roommates made a gesture, offering me a hit. I shook my head no.

"Was my mother here?" I asked breathlessly. I was holding the Louisville Slugger in both hands, like a batter waiting for a pitch.

"Oh man, dude, was your mother here!" exclaimed the roommate in the lawn chair. He and the other roommate giggled, but not Lance.

"Look," Lance began unsteadily, "I told your mother I was sorry, I've told you I'm sorry. About the tooth. And about the gun. It wasn't even loaded, man, I swear to God." Both of the roommates burst out in uncontrollable laughter at this point. Lance stared up at me.

"Rick, man, your mom is……" He stopped short. The roommates were hysterical now, writhing in laughter. The one holding the bong had just taken a hit and now he was coughing violently.

"My mom is what?"

"Your mom is…..strong. Man, she is strong for her size." More hysteria from the peanut gallery.

Lance told me my mother had gone to see his mother, who, he said, lived just two houses up from Stevie's.

Less than ten minutes later I'd parked my bug in front of the McLaughlin residence. Halfway to the front door I spotted my mother through the kitchen window. She was sitting with another woman. They were drinking coffee and smoking cigarettes. My mother said something and the other woman laughed. "Well, my work here is done", I whispered in self-mocking sarcasm and turned back to the street.

The McLaughlins, of course, paid for a new crown. And I received a letter from Lance in the mail telling me one last time that he was sorry about 'the tooth'. No mention of the gun this time, but he signed with a 'Sincerely'. I don't know what transpired that day between Millie and Lance. I'll never know what he meant by the 'strong' comment. Nor do I know anything about the conversation between Lance's mother and mine. I never asked. My sister and I had a saying when we where growing up—'Let sleeping moms lie'.

The Rock
January 2008

A week from today I'll be sixty years old, but I swear I'm a nineteen-year-old kid trapped in a downwardly spiraling body. In many ways I still think like a nineteen-year-old, though a little bit wiser; have the same tastes, though a trifle less extravagant; and have the same sense of humor, with maybe a little more understanding of the irony that makes things funny. And fortunately, it seems that the older I get, the easier it is to slip back in time, slip back to nineteen, to nine, to junior high wood shop. It's like I grew up, hit adulthood, and in order to make a living and raise a family without distractions, I just sort of put the first twenty years of my life in archive. Now, with two grown boys and the freedom that comes from working not because you have to but because you want to, the files so carefully catalogued come tumbling out with just the slightest provocation.

Take this morning. Barreling down the foothills to a work day in the flatlands, I listened to a Chinese peasant's account of the terrible pollution being caused by the huge Three Gorges Reservoir nearly completed on the Yangtze River. Through a translator, the poor fisherman described in agonizing detail the yellow sludge being pumped into the new body of water by a chemical plant. Not accidentally escaping from the plant; methodically and aggressively being PUMPED into the river.

And in a nanosecond I am whisked away to the jarring racket of a jack-hammer engaged in mortal conflict with a forty inch thick slab of concrete, nine feet wide, about thirty feet long and straddling a little creek with just a trickle of sulfur-smelling water. I lean hard into the bucking hammer and let go a tumult of blows, each opening a new but ever so slight fissure in the 'Rock'. That's what we call it even though it doesn't look like a rock. But it's hard as a rock and stubborn as a rock and on this hot afternoon in June of 1967 the Rock seems to taunt, 'Are you kidding? Move me from where I've lain for forty years? You chumps must be out of your mind.'

I let go the handles of the jackhammer and it bumps a last sputter and goes silent. My ears ring and my hands tingle like they're wired to a car battery.

"Okay, Doyle, all yours." My partner moves in and begins removing the chunks of slab I've broken up. He heaves each piece into a small, iron dumpster next to the demolition. I light a cigarette, sit down in the shade and look westward, beyond the salt flats, across the San Francisco Bay, at the purplish coastal mountains above San Mateo.

"I don't get this. I just don't get it. It almost seems like they're having us do this just to have us do something. Something back-breaking. And did you get the expression on Moe's face when I asked him why we were removing a buried monolith of concrete and re-bar in the middle of nowhere?"

Doyle looks over his shoulder at me and then spits on the ground.

"Let go of it, man. Just let go of it. What the f___ difference does it make, anyways? They could have us doing this, or that, or any other damned thing, and you know what, that's what we'd be doing; exactly what we were told to do. Just let go of it."

Doyle had been right. It was the first week in July and I'd be there until the third week in August and it really didn't make any difference what they had me doing—jack hammering, digging a ditch, stacking pallets, cleaning silos. It just didn't matter. I would work eight exhausting hours per day for nine weeks, I'd take the money, (very good money for a nineteen year old in the late sixties), and I'd hightail it back to college. Nine weeks out of my life, not a big deal even then. (Barely an instant now.)

Doyle was a different case altogether. I'd snapped up the high paying summer job at FMC's Chemical Division, in Newark, because I knew it was a quick in-and-out way to make tuition money. Doyle Mc Ginty, a year younger than me, was there for the long haul. He'd begun working at the plant a year before and would be working there long after I'd returned to San Jose State. Doyle was tall, buff, a very good-looking guy with shoulder-length hair tied in a pony-tail, many rough edges and a good ol' boy, a party-hearty dude. He used poor grammar and thought reading was for sissies; but, although a high school dropout, there was nothing stupid about my partner; he lacked book learning and was proud of it.

"Okay," he grinned, "your turn, Huggie." (Huggie was the nickname I was given the very first day I came to work at FMC-ChemD. Short for tree-hugging hippie environmentalist…..it's true, the term 'tree-hugger' goes at least that far back.)

Next day, we switched; Doyle handled the jackhammer and I tossed the concrete remnants into the dumpster. And so it went for the next two weeks—hammer, clean up, hammer, clean up. Very slow going, despite the fact that we were both hard workers. Three and a half feet of solid concrete is, well, three and a half feet of concrete.

One mid-morning about two weeks into the assault on the Rock, our supervisor, Moe Avila, drove his golf cart out to the isolated spot where Doyle and I were working. Moe waited till my jack hammering went silent and then said, "Come on, boys, hop on. We've got somethin' real special for you." Moe grinned a sadist's smile, I shuddered but Doyle, in pure McGinty style, spit and said, "Sure, whatever."

"Moe," I asked as we headed back toward the main part of the plant, "would this special something have anything to do with the silos?" I knew about the dreaded silos.

"Guess we'll just have to wait and see about that, won't we Huggie?" Though Doyle clearly didn't hold my 'college-boy' status against me (his reaction ranged somewhere between indifference and mild curiosity); Moe, on the other hand, most assuredly did. A short, stout Portuguese man in his late 50's who'd spent the past 30 years moving up the corporate ladder from ditch-digger/ jack hammerer like Doyle and me to supervisor of ditch-diggers/

jack hammerers with beat up old golf cart, he clearly had no use for a coddled college boy (though I was not what you'd call an intellectual by any stretch), especially one whose dad had helped wrangle the summer job at excellent union wages. (My pop had worked at the plant since before I was born; he was a maintenance man and a Class A welder. While it was true he'd helped me get the job, 'getting your kid on at the plant' for a summer was pretty much a tradition there. Moe knew that, but there was something about my returning to college in the fall that rubbed him the wrong way.)

Sure enough, Moe Avila drove us straight through and into the opposite end of the plant to the South Silo complex, a series of six fifty-five foot steel silos used for storing calcite and feldspar, the two abrasives used for the production of industrial cleansers manufactured by FMC-ChemD.

"Jack says you two have three days, starting tomorrow, to scrub one through six. All of 'em are empty, or will be by tomorrow. That's two a day. On Friday we'll have three rail cars coming in to fill 'em, so you got Tuesday, Wednesday and Thursday. Jack'll be here first thing Friday morning to inspect 'em. Got it?"

"Got it, Moe-Man. Where's our stuff?" Doyle knew the drill. He'd dangled his turn the summer before. And now it was my turn, and Moe loved it.

Moe pointed to a corrugated shack next to Silo One. Doyle jumped out, walked over to the shack and immediately started throwing our equipment out. Leather harness, respirator, goggles and a shovel……everything we'd need to scrape off the inside walls of six fifty-five foot silos. I felt sick.

Doyle and I ate our lunch together everyday, outside, on the porch, not in the lunchroom with the regular, older guys. (In most respects, my partner and I were light years away: he the tough guy, the bad dude, the fighter; me the college boy, the tree-hugger, the literature major who'd never been in a fight his entire life. But in a few ways we were from the same mold: confident, used to being the alpha dog, bigger than life. Why or however it happened, the contrasts and similarities equaled out and we'd become pals in a few short weeks, albeit a tentative palship.)

Most days I just listened to my partner talk about his drug deals, his crazy roommates and their nightly parties, and of course always, about his girlfriend Carol. I'd decided in my first year of college that I'd be a writer, maybe a novelist, and so pulling stories and facts and descriptions out of people and then filing them away had become sort of second nature to me. I was always asking questions. In fact, he talked so much about Carol I felt like I knew her. Beautiful brunette, huge brown eyes, dating Doyle since her freshman year in high school, gorgeous enough to be a model. It seemed to me that Doyle was more proud of his girl than anything else in his life. Really, what else was there? A drop out, a dead-end job, selling nickel bags of grass…..but Carol, Carol was something special. She was a goddess and she was going to college, or would be starting in September, and she was Doyle's girl.

But on this particular day we didn't talk about our personal lives, we talked about scrubbing the silo.

"Did I mention I have a fear of heights?"

"Yeah," Doyle said, "you've mentioned that three times since the Moe-Man took us over to the silos. Huggie man, you've got to go with the flow. Or maybe this time, float with the flow." He laughed and I tried to laugh with him.

Doyle was referring to the fact that the scrubber of the silo walls wore a heavy leather harness, was lowered down into the fifty-foot storage tank on a cable using an electric winch and then dangled there, swinging from side to side, scraping the stuck on calcite and feldspar with the highest-tech tool available, a shovel. And, of course, with each whack by the shovel, a fine dust would be exploded into the chamber making it harder to see and, worse, harder to breathe. I knew all this because my dad had told me many times about the scraping of the silos. He'd done it once, way back when he started at the plant. Nowadays, he'd told me, they used the 'summer kids' for that job.

Doyle and I spent the rest of the day hammering away at the Rock. We were told to meet the next morning at the silo complex, but when I got there just Moe was waiting.

"So" he jeered, "I hear pony-tail got into a little trouble last night. Called in from Santa Rita this morning." (Santa Rita was the name of the County Jail.)

"Doyle got arrested?" I asked. My first thought was drug bust. My partner and his roommates (shack mates, really—they lived in a falling-down cabin along Niles Creek east of Fremont) dealt marijuana by the bag. Very small time.

"Yep, disturbing the peace is what they charged him with. I guess he made quite a ruckus at his girl's house last night. Parents called the sheriff. Anyway, no silo swingin' today, Huggie. Jack's gonna be P.O.'d?] and that's a fact. Jump on and I'll take you back over to your hammer. You're on your own today, college boy."

As we bumped along the gravel road through the center of the plant and then out toward the bay and my giant concrete slab, I remember feeling relieved that I wouldn't be descending into a silo that day.

"So, Moe, when will they let Doyle out? When's he coming back?"

"Dunno", Moe replied without looking over at me. "But you better hope he's back soon because if he ain't here tomorrow, it'll be me running the winch for you on silo one and not pony tail. I ain't had to climb up there in ten years, if I have to do it tomorrow I'm not going to be in no good mood."

We drove the rest of the way in silence. When I got off, Moe immediately started to drive away on his golf cart.

"Hey, Moe," I called. He stopped.

"Why was it you said they were having us break up this big old slab of cement?"

"I didn't," he said, and sped off.

I spent the entire day there alone, jack-hammering chunks off the rock, clearing them away, and then jack-hammering some more. I can remember the feel of the jack-hammering after forty years, I can remember hearing the songs KFRC was playing on the transistor radio—Ode to Billy Joe, Light My Fire, Respect,

Groovin', All You Need is Love—I can even remember the kind of tennis shoes I was wearing. But I can't remember much about what I was thinking…..you know, what I was thinking about with respect to my life at that time. I know I didn't have a girl friend at the time so that had to be a constant source of angst—I had two or three I was working on but it was slow going. (One was a former high school sweetheart, now a senior, with whom I'd had a rocky relationship for nearly three years; the other was a girl from another town with whom I couldn't seem to make much headway. She was shockingly gorgeous, way prettier than I was handsome, but I'd convinced myself that she could love me for my mind.) And I was worried about making enough money to get through another year of school. In truth, the only thing I'm certain filled my thoughts that day was a vision of Moe with his hands on the controls of the electric winch that would lower me into and lift me out of silo number one. Doyle just HAD to be back the next day.

And he did come to work the next day and, oh, what a foul mood he was in.

"So, Doyle, what the hell happened?" I asked.

"Nothin'! Let's just do this," which was easy for him to say since I was the one going into the silo. My partner helped me on with the harness, then the respirator mask, then the goggles, and then we climbed the fifty foot steel ladder to the top of Silo #1 where he attached the quarter-inch winch cable to my harness.

"Have fun," Doyle said, handing me a shovel.

I dangled in Silo #1 for two hours and fifteen minutes that first morning, scraping encrusted detergent abrasives off the steel walls. The experience was the worst of my nineteen-year life, and of course I had no way of knowing that it would be trumped by an even worse experience right after lunch.

At noon we were sitting at our table outside the breakroom. My eyes were burning like hot embers, I was hoarse and I had a fine white dusting of calcite and feldspar from the top of my head to my sneakers. As workers wandered past on their way into lunch—all of them knew what I'd been doing that morning- each one would walk by, take one look at me and make some comment. A few encouraging, some taunting, mostly just blue collar guys being blue collar guys with a fellow blue collar guy.

"So," I asked leaning across the table in a hushed voice, "What happened with you, man? They said you were in jail."

Doyle drew deeply on his Camel, which, of course, had no filter.

"Yup," he said with a grimace, "I sure was. Man oh man, I f____ed up. Big time!" He sighed and took another drag.

"I went over to Carol's the night before last and while I was there I found out she's been cheatin' on me. I just went nutso, man, psycho, you know what I'm sayin'? You ever been so mad you just start breaking things?"

"What kind of things?"

"You know, man, things. We were in her bedroom….you know, like her clock radio. Her hair dryer. S___ like that."

"You caught her with another guy?" I asked in amazement. (Needless to say I'd never been mad enough to break a clock radio or a hair dryer.)

"No, I didn't actually catch her with the guy. In a way, it was worse. Carol went to get us some cokes and while she was out of the room I found a letter from the chump. A friggin' love letter! Can you believe that? I swear to God if the guy would a' been there I'd have killed him dead. The dude is lucky. He's lucky, man".

Doyle was getting worked up as he spoke. He looked about to explode.

"Hey, man, calm down. Doyle, man, you know how you're always telling me to be cool? Well, I'm telling you, be cool. You can work this thing out. You just have to talk it through. And not break anything else. Did she cop to it? Admit it?"

"Hell, no," he barked, "she swears he's just some guy she knows and they write letters to each other but that's it. Just friends. I say bull-s___. BULL-S___!"

"Well, maybe she's telling the truth. Did you ever think of that?" I felt for my partner. I knew he was crazy about this girl and now some jerk was trying to steal her away.

"Yeah, actually I DID think of that. Until I read the f____ing letter he sent to her. "Here," he said, read this," and handed me a folded wad he took out of his jeans. Then, just as quickly, he pulled it back. "No, that ain't right. You shouldn't see this." He closed his eyes. "Man oh man oh man, what am I gonna do? I can't lose my baby. I can't. And now she won't even talk to me. And her old man had me thrown in jail and says if I set foot on his property he's gonna get a 'straining order. Man oh man, what am I gonna do?"

"I'll tell you what you're gonna do," Moe said approaching our table, "you're gonna get your asses back to #1. Lunch break is over." He looked at me and scowled, "Cornish, you clean that mask out before you go back down there. Pony-tail will show you where the filters are. Put a new one in. You breathe any of that xylene sulfonate in and your lungs are gonna feel like they're in Satan's hell."

I re-entered Silo #1 like a condemned man being lowered into a gas chamber. Two words pounded in my skull…."xylene sulfonate"….."xylene sulfonate". Nobody, not even my dad, had mentioned xylene sulfonate before.

I'd been scraping for maybe half an hour when Doyle yelled down to stop. It took a moment for the echoing to fade away. "Yeah," I said, "what's up?"

"I been thinkin'. You should read this damned letter. To tell you the truth, I don't understand all the words in it. And it's written sort of like a, you know, like a poem. Not like with rhymes, but, you know, like a poem."

"You mean blank verse," I said through the mask.

"I dunno, it's just got some words I've never heard before, and it's got words I have heard before that don't seem to go together. You know what I'm sayin'?"

"No," I coughed, "not really. Like what?" As I dangled from the steel cable I could just barely see Doyle's face through the dust. He was at least twenty-five feet above me.

"Okay, well listen to this. 'I watched as she waited with almost a close, almost a close toward me, and I couldn't not watch as she waited, with an almost close, do you see?' Now what the hell does that mean?"

"Doyle", I asked, trying with every ounce of energy, every scrap of courage, to sound nonchalant, "Did this prick sign his name to the letter?"

"Uh, yeah. Yeah. Hang on….let me see." I could hear the shuffling of paper.

"Here it is. Rick. His name is Rick. Just like yours."

(About twenty years later I told this story to a group of my colleagues at lunch one day. That afternoon one of my employees, a bright young statistician and demographer named Nancy Anderson, came into my office and glibly announced, "Here, I've worked these numbers up for you. Let me know if you have any questions." The sheet was titled "Probability, or LACK THEREOF, Of Chance Couplings as Described at 3/14/88 Staff Lunch," and it laid out U.S. Census data pulled for 1965 for the County of Alameda. 289,458 people between the ages of 5 and 19 lived in the county in '65 (the closest Nancy could get to the actual year of the incident, 1967) and, using an algorithm we employed back then for projecting school enrollments, she calculated that there would have been roughly 35,000 eighteen-to-nineteen year old boys and girls living in the county then. Given the fact that Carol and Doyle and I lived in three separate towns, each at least thirty miles away from the other two, it was not unreasonable for Nancy to run her probability table using the entire county population of 18-19 year olds. While I don't remember the exact odds that Nancy derived from the census numbers, I do remember distinctly that I'd had a 84% better chance of winning the Bay Meadows Exacta for 50 days in a row than I did for choosing my co-worker's girlfriend to hit on.)

Before Doyle began reading the lines of the poem I'd sent to his girl friend Carol, I couldn't have imagined any circumstance in which I would have chosen dangling from a steel cable in a dust storm of carcinogens over standing free and unfettered in the sunlight. And yet there I was, thanking God that I was down here and Doyle was up there and he couldn't read my face.

"Okay, well I'll take a look when I come up. Right now I wanna get this job done so I can get out of this hell hole."

"Thanks, Rick," Doyle said, his voice cracking just a bit. I remember thinking how odd that sounded coming from my partner.

What Carol had told Doyle about her pen pal was technically true. We were just friends and had never actually dated. More like, you could say, hung out a few times. But the truth was, she and I had been doing the dance, mostly through the mail, and it was just a matter of time before I would have hooked and reeled. She was tired of her boyfriend, she said, a tough rebel type, very macho, a nasty temper, inarticulate. A sweet guy but just not……sensitive. Unlike me, the college student with plans of being a professional writer, already a self-proclaimed poet and with enough sensitivity to buy Carol a single red rose for her birthday. She was feeling torn, she said, which caused me to feel encouraged. What I was definitely not feeling was even a sub-atomic particle of guilt or remorse about the boyfriend. Not until, of course, I put the generic boyfriend together with a name and a face. Now I felt terrible.

During our afternoon break, Doyle gave me the letter he'd found two nights before in his girlfriend's bedroom. We sat at our picnic table outside the break room, I reading the three pages thoughtfully, studiously; he watching me read.

"Well," I said, taking a deep pull on my cigarette and looking past Doyle, off into the distance, "I'd say you've got nothing to worry about. This guy, this Rick, is obviously a dork. Zero competition for you."

"You don't think that's a love letter, man? How many times does the word 'love' need to be in a letter before it's a love letter?"

"Not letter, Doyle, love poem. It's a poem, man, and not even a good one. Don't you see, this dork's a wanna-be poet. Can you even imagine a chick like Carol goin' for a wimp like this?"

"Hey, you said you write poetry in college. Does that make you a wimp?"

I didn't like where this was going.

"Look," I said, "let it go, man. Call Carol and apologize for losing your cool. Tell her you believe her. Burn this friggin' letter and forget it. You two are in love, right? So tell her you love her. Buy her some roses, red ones. Now come on, let's get back to the friggin' silo."

"Wow, man, it sounds like you're starting to dig on going down in there."

"Very funny," I snapped. He had no idea how much I wanted to get back down there.

It took us two weeks to finish the silos. Each day Doyle had a little less to say about the letter and his wimp rival. Halfway through the job, a new kid, another college student, got hired onto the yard crew, Doyle was reassigned to work with the regular, older maintenance crew (he'd graduated) and the new guy was made my new partner. Jerry was a Phys-Ed major at Cal State Hayward; a small, wiry Portuguese kid. His very first day, I lowered him into silo #4 to scrape. I didn't see Doyle much the rest of that summer. (And never heard from, tried to contact, wrote to, or received mail from Carol. I don't know if she ever became aware of the bizarre coincidence that had brought her and me and Doyle together for a brief time.)

Jerry and I were given various odd jobs, mostly clean-up kinds of things, but between jobs we'd always return to our ongoing assignment, that of destroying the 'Rock'. Jerry was quite a bit smaller than me, so I did all the jack hammering and he, all the concrete removal. I liked it better that way. Unlike Doyle, my new partner shared my curiosity about the slab. Why would a humongous slab of concrete out in the boondocks have to be removed? There was nothing out there but salt ponds, and beyond that, the bay.

Near the end of the summer, in early August, we hit metal, which turned out to be a corrugated culvert, three-feet in diameter, that was buried under those forty inches of concrete. I remember we whooped and hollered like we'd hit pay dirt, even though neither of us had known there was anything to hit. In another two weeks, we'd completely exposed the pipe and, on my last day of work, a crane was brought over to pull the thirty-foot pipe out of the ground. It was kind of a big deal: along with us and the crane operator, Moe, Moe's boss Jack, Jack's boss, the plant superintendent Mr. Danielson, and a couple of "suits" were on hand.

What I'd suspected all summer long to have been nothing more than a make-work job now seemed to have grown legs. Jerry and I stood about thirty yards away from the corroded pipe, toward the salt ponds, as the crane was brought into position. The two guys in suits, both studying blueprints they'd rolled out on the ground, stood opposite us on the other side of the ditch and Moe and Jack and Mr. Danielson were right there at the edge of the trench, where the crane was headed. Danielson turned and walked toward Dennis [Jerry?] and me; Moe and Jack lagged behind.

"You're Vance Cornish's boy, right?" he asked, looking directly at me.

"Right, that's me."

"You know how long I've known your pop?" he asked, and then before I could answer he went on, "well, it took the whole summer, but you got her uncovered. Good work, boys." He patted Jerry on the back. I was astonished that the superintendent of the plant, the big, big boss, would know about our stupid jack hammering project.

"Yep," I said, "we sure did get her uncovered. But, Mr. Danielson, I was just wondering, well, I was just wondering why the pipe needed to be dug out. What was the reason?"

Danielson looked puzzled.

"Jack, you never told your crew why we're pulling the pipe?" he asked, looking a bit annoyed.

"Yeah, well, er, no…..I mean, I dunno. MOE?"

"Sure I told 'em. Of course. I said, now you boys has got to get this culvert outta here by the end of the summer 'cause Jack, he wants it outta here." The Moe-Man looked proud of himself. Jack was squirming.

Danielson let out a weary sigh. "Here's what I think, boys. Here's what my management philosophy is: we're all a team here, even the summer boys. And everyone on the team shares the same goals, you know, the same objectives. If you don't know what those goals and objectives are, that is, if you don't know why you're doing what you're doing, how can anybody expect you to do a good job. Right?"

Jerry said, "Right!"

I asked, "So why did we dig up the big pipe?"

"Flow", Jack said, "to increase flow. See this ditch that runs underneath the road through the culvert and out to the salt ponds? We shut it down last year till we could increase the size of the culvert. We'll get a new six-footer in, and by October we can open her up again. We'll double capacity."

"Capacity of what?" I asked naively.

"Of run-off into the ponds, and eventually into the bay," Superintendent Danielson said flatly.

"Run-off?"

"Sure, run-off. You know, waste, the stuff that's left after we make the product. It's got to go somewhere, doesn't it?"

Even forty years ago, at nineteen, I was the kind of person who always had a comeback, but not this time. I just looked at Danielson, and then beyond him at the salt flats and then way out at the San Francisco Bay. The summer had sped by, I'd made some good money and I'd learned a few things.

Almost Banjo
June 2003

I wish I could say I'd listened to Uncle Red play his banjo when I was growing up….could tell you how he'd pull it out during family get-togethers and just light up the room playing all the old mountain favorites all night long. But the truth is, I think I only heard him play it once, and that was very late at night when I'd gotten up in my jammies searching for a drink of water and wandered into a grownup party. There was Red, the center of attention, playing and singing, with his charming, boozy, mischievous trademark smile.

Uncle Red was the sixth of eleven children, my dad was seventh and they were only ten months apart. The eleven Cornish kids and their mother, Maude, lived in a sod shack on the Nebraska plains. The father, my grandfather, was an itinerant Baptist minister, banjo player and alcoholic whose busy touring ministry brought him home just often and long enough to make more little Cornish's. My grandmother and her eleven children were very, very poor, but somehow the family made it, season after season. Most of the stories my father told me about his growing up fell into two categories—how their plains family survived with hard work and luck and how my Uncle Red drove my grandma crazy. There was the time she and the nine other kids went into town on the buggy, leaving my dad and Red to slop the single family hog and how, instead of feeding it, ten year old Red got it into his head he was going to butcher the hog as a surprise for their mama and broke off the blade of a butcher knife in its neck, in the house…..'oh, my God, Ricky, the blood, the blood', my dad would say. Or the time he was sent into town for a bag of flour and returned home with a brand new Gibson banjo. Or the time he talked my father into making cabbage and carrot wine in an old abandoned farmhouse down the road. It was after Red started making wine, and later liquor, that the stories really got wild.

So, uncle Red was the family screw up, the one who always got into trouble, the one who could charm the wrist watch right off you, who could play any musical instrument and who, in his early twenties, figured he'd rob from the rich by pulling a bank job in Belfush, South Dakota with an unloaded pellet gun. The bank teller, a few years older and much bigger than Uncle Red, didn't even bother reading the note. He just broke Red's nose with a single punch and my uncle was carted off to jail. Silly unloaded pellet gun not withstanding, bank robbery was by then a federal offense and Red went to jail with the big dogs in Minneapolis for just under five years.

By the time Uncle Red got out of the slammer, most of the Cornish clan, including my dad, who was by then married to my mom, had gone off to California to work in the shipyards in Alameda—America was gearing up for war and jobs were plentiful and good-paying out west. In fact, here in California is where the entire Cornish brood settled into their own little families and made their new lives. And it's interesting as I look back now.… they all had very small families. The largest was our family, with two kids. Most of my father's siblings had one or no children. I guess it was like, after you've stretched fried flour and cabbage soup twelve ways for so many years, you just want to keep the number of mouths to a minimum.

Red hung around the Black Hills for a while, got his old high school girlfriend, Florence, pregnant, got into another scrape with the law and, with great encouragement from the local magistrate, took his new little family out west. (Uncle Red and aunt Florence would eventually divorce, re-marry, divorce, re-marry, divorce and live together unmarried for the remainder of their lives). What kept the two of them together was their son, Little Harold, a beautiful redheaded boy, (and later an eye-poppingly handsome young man with his dad's silver tongue). In fact, it was Little Harold's appearance on the scene that got Red on the straight and narrow, or at least as straight and as narrow as he could be and still booze heavily, gamble and womanize.

Little Harold was the apple of his parents' eye. They lived for him. He was a lot like his dad.…red-haired, charming, a natural musician, and always, always in trouble. First in school, later with the law. I remember so well the day he died. I was ten and we were packing our 55 Chrysler getting ready for a one-week vacation in Clear Lake. The phone rang, my mother answered and almost at once she began crying. It was aunt Florence. The police had found Little Harold, just one week out of county jail, shot up with an overdose of heroin by dealers against whom he'd turned state's evidence. No Clear Lake for my family that week, which,

I must admit, for this ten year old was just barely less devastating than the loss of a loved one.

For the next thirty years it would be the loss of their son that would keep Red and Florence together. They would alternately hate themselves and one another for what happened to Little Harold.

Fast forward twenty years. My dad calls me one Saturday morning. "I've, ah, got something for you," he says a bit cryptically, "Red gave me something for you. Don't say anything to your mother. Just invite us over for dinner. Okay?" I knew Uncle Red had been in the hospital with a serious heart problem. "Sure," I said, "come tonight." When I told my wife about the call, she asked what my uncle could possibly want me to have.

"I'll bet it's his old banjo. I'll bet that's what it is. But don't say anything….there's something about my mom not knowing."

"But why would your mother object to your having a banjo?" Claudia asked.

"She objects to EVERYTHING connected in any way to Red," I explained.

After dinner that Saturday night my father announces he's out of smokes. "Come on, Ricky, go for a ride with me." My mother's in the kitchen helping with dishes, oblivious. Two blocks from the house my dad pull's to the side of the road and parks. "So what's up," I ask, "what's this about Uncle Red?" "Well," my father begins tentatively, "Red's been real, real sick. His heart's giving out. You know, my brother's lived a damned hard life, a damned fast life.

So he's in the hospital and his doctor says he's not gonna make it. So….." my dad has a pained expression now. This isn't easy for him. "So, I visited with Red in the hospital last week and he says to me, you know, Bebe, your boy's the last….the last man. All us kids, and all our kids, and it'll come down to Ricky to carry on the Cornish name. And then he asked me to give you this." My father reaches under the seat and pulls out a towel tied in a bundle with a string. Definitely not a banjo.

"Here" he says.

I pull the string off and unwrap the towel. There, in my hands, is a .32 caliber pistol, snub nosed, only good for two things—killing at close range or threatening to kill at close range. "It was Little Harold's," my dad whispers, explaining what I'd already guessed. "I told him I didn't want you to have it. That it was just crazy that he'd kept it all these years. But you know Red….he was determined. And it's pretty sure he's dying. So now you've got it and I've kept my promise. I think you should throw it away, but that's up to you."

I've still got the 32. Red lived another twenty years, outliving my father by ten. In fact, he outlived all of his brothers and sisters. Don't know whatever happened to that Gibson banjo….just know I didn't get it.

Post Script

Eight years after writing this account, at the publication of this collection of stories in 2011, the pistol is languishing in a gun shop in Jackson, waiting for me to call the owner and give the go ahead to repair it. My friend, J.D. Rhynes, the small arms devotee who took it in for me, says it'll cost more than its worth to make it 'shootable'. "Only worth it if'n for the sentimental value", J.D. says. Oddly, I think I'll have the gun repaired. Go figure.

I Like to Cook A Lot A Lot
January 2004

I enjoy cooking a lot a lot. Which is to say I enjoy cooking lots of food for lots of people. I'm told I do pretty well cooking for large groups, but that's not always been the case.

Mid way into adulthood, I'd never cooked at all. I was a wood worker and loved spending time in my shop. When in the mid 1970's my first wife and I split up, I moved into a small apartment and lost access to a wood shop for a time. Quickly growing restless with no way to create with my hands, I turned to my apartment's kitchen and learned to cook. Luckily for my friends and family, I mostly cooked for myself in the early, experimental days.

I was put off by cookbooks in much the same way I'd steered clear of plans and blueprints in my shop. I would eat something in a restaurant and then go home and experiment over and over and over again until it tasted good….not necessarily like the restaurant food, but good. This was not exactly a quick way to learn to cook, and there were some pretty ugly meals strewn along the road to culinary success, but eventually this trial and error process worked—people began liking my cooking. The more I cooked, the more people I cooked for, the more positive feedback I got. (I've been told by a psychologist friend of mine that my primary, de-fault motivator is pleasing those around me. Try convincing my wife of that.)

In late summer, 1980, my first real chance to do something really big cooking-wise came up. I'd had a jam at my house (by then I was out of the apartment and had a shop again, but cooking was now my number one avocation) and I prepared a sit down meal for the whole lot of us. Cajun cooking….jambalaya, dirty rice, ribs. It was a feast. A couple folks attended who happened to be officers of the Santa Cruz Bluegrass Society and, after dinner, I approached them with a proposal—how about instead of doing the traditional potluck at the SCBS annual Fall Campout, I cook a Cajun meal for everyone. Each person would pay a few bucks to cover costs, the food would be great and folks could avoid the hassle of bringing the usual potatoes salad and baked beans to the potluck. "But can you cook for that many people," one of them asked? "Sure I can," I said without hesitation, "no problem." They said yes.

There's not much I've learned well enough in life that qualifies me to give advice, but here's one piece I feel confident sharing: If you're just starting out as a cook, don't make your first large meal a dinner for 300 people. Start smaller and build up to it. We started food prep the day before—there were five of us—I was in charge and I had four helpers, none who knew anything about cooking for large numbers, all who thought I was nuts. For my part, I was the picture of confidence. The meal would be simple—a wonderful, spicy sausage and shrimp and chicken Jambalaya, crusty sour dough rolls and a nice, healthy green salad. I'd served that same meal to as many as 10 people before. What could go wrong?

Okay, so here's what could and did go wrong. Because I was an inexperienced cook and relied on intuition alone, I intuited that the way to make Jambalaya for 300 people instead of 10 people was to just multiply all the ingredients times thirty. This, I learned, was only partly true. Yes, you need 30 times more sausage, shrimp, chicken, tomatoes, etc., but you most certainly don't need 30 times more cayenne pepper and Tabasco sauce. That's just not how it works.

By late in the afternoon of the day of the event we were busy filling huge aluminum serving pans with the jambalaya when one of the workers tasted it. It was my friend, Bill Schneiderman.

"Holy Cow," he winced, "did you taste this," Bill was fanning his mouth.

"Of course I tasted it," I lied. Once I got a recipe down, I never tasted as I went….it just seemed like bad luck to me. "It's supposed to be spicy. It's Cajun food. Remember? Cajun!" I told Bill not to worry and, to be honest, I wasn't worried. Billy didn't have a tolerance for spicy hot food, and besides, I'd followed my own recipe to the letter. Thirty times everything. What could go wrong?

It was two years before I attended another SCBS event. It's not that I was afraid to….after all, it wasn't like I'd done anything malicious or on purpose. And I took the entire financial loss myself. And several people told me the salad and rolls were delicious, though not exactly filling. And late that night of the campout, a swarm of perhaps thirty raccoons descended on the Jambalaya, which had been left out on a picnic table, and in twenty minutes it was completely gone (they even ate two pot holders)—so really, no food went to waste. No, I certainly wasn't afraid to show my face to the South Bay bluegrass community…I just felt I needed to let things, well, cool off a bit.

By 1982, with two more years of cooking under my belt and memories of the Jambalaya gone wrong fading, I felt it was time to take back my reputation. I hatched another, and ultimately much more dangerous, scheme. I'd become good friends with Paul Lampert, owner of Paul's Saloon in San Francisco's Marina District. From the 70's to the 90's Paul's Saloon was without question the number one bluegrass venue on the West Coast—everyone from Monroe to the Osborn's to Stanley to Skaggs and Rice had played on Paul's stage. One Saturday night during a Grass Menagerie break, Paul and I sat sipping beers at the bar. As was frequently the case, Paul was grousing about how terrible business was, how people just didn't appreciate good bluegrass music, didn't appreciate him, etc.

"Dammit, whaddah they want from me….do they want my blood? Do they want my bones and my blood?"

"You know what this place needs," I suddenly asked on impulse, without thinking a moment of what I was saying, "it needs AN EVENT. Paul's Saloon needs an annual event, something to get people excited…..to look forward to all year long."

"No," Paul snapped. "I don't even know what you're talking about, but no." Imagine the meanest, most ill tempered, crankiest, cross, sarcastic, Bluto-like person you've ever known in your life. Now imagine ten of those people kneaded and molded together and then rolled out into a single, frightening human form, huge, overalls-clad, ghostly white beard, sulky eyes behind thick horn-rimmed glasses, loud and perpetually angry voice….that was Paul Lampert. And in 1982 I was proud to call him my friend.

"No, really", I said a bit unsteadily, "what we need to do is throw a First Annual Paul's Saloon Barbeque and Bluegrass Blowout."

"WE?", he nearly screamed, "WE! You got a mouse in your pocket? This is my bar and I make the decisions!" And then he did scream—"NO!"

And so that night, after several more beers and some Sake at the Sushi place around the corner from the Saloon, we began planning the first ever Paul's Saloon Barbeque and Bluegrass Blowout. By now I was an expert when it came to making Cajun-style chicken gumbo, so we'd serve that, along with Cajun-style potato salad, Cajun hot links and sour dough sandwich rolls. I would front the money and get paid back when the receipts came in on the day of the event, we'd charge seven bucks a meal and split the profit. I would do all of the food prep, grilling and serving. The big event would take place on a Sunday afternoon two months hence—that would give us time to publicize it. Paul would hire High Country, more or less the house band, and my group, the Grass Menagerie, would open for Butch and the boys. Even Paul, the crankiest, most pessimistic human being in the history of mankind, was a little excited, though he made every effort to hide it. And why wouldn't he be excited? We had a good plan. What could go wrong?

The next morning when I told my wife Lynn about the scheme (we'd been married only a short time at that point and she was not yet able to read my mind) she had a few questions: What if instead of a profit, there was a loss? Why would I want to work so hard to help such an unpleasant man? How would I know how many people to cook for? Who was I going to get to help me do all the work—not her? Where was I going to prepare all this food—not her kitchen? And finally, was I completely, totally out of my mind?

Of all the memories I have of the two days leading up to the First Annual Paul's Saloon Barbeque and Bluegrass Blowout—running over Lynn's planter of daisies as I backed my truck up the driveway to off load the boxes and boxes of food into the kitchen, my friend, Marilyn the Nurse, slicing her finger open as she cleaned and chopped up fifty pounds of chicken, blowing out the garbage disposal mid way through the operation, completely destroying our refrigerator--the one that stands out the most is the last bit of food prep done in the wee hours the night before the event. By then my four helpers had drifted off home, Lynn had gone to bed and there I was mixing up the last of the Cajun potato salad in the kitchen sink. Yes, an entire sink full of potato salad, and I was mixing it with my hands, my arms buried up past my elbows, when suddenly the cayenne pepper that had floated thickly in the air all day long got to me. I had to sneeze. There, at that critical moment, when so much hung in the balance, I too wondered—was I completely, totally out of my mind?

By noon the next day things were looking a lot better. We'd transported all the food—dozens of half-gallon milk cartons full of gumbo and potato salad—all the equipment--grills, utensils, paper plates--everything to San Francisco from San Jose. All my helpers had arrived and we were set up with serving tables and two big grills on the sidewalk in front of the saloon. Paul was in great spirits, barely screaming at anyone, and had even put on a Hawaiian shirt under his overalls. And Lynn was gradually getting into the spirit of the event—on the drive up I'd promised to replace our refrigerator the very next day. Yes, all was right with the world…the fog and clouds were beginning to burn off the Marina….customers were actually beginning to show up….. we'd begin serving in an hour and I was all ready to light off the charcoal. And that's when a black and white pulled up to the curb.

"What are you doing?" asked the patrolman as he got out of his cruiser.

"What am I doing?" It was pretty obvious what I was doing since I held a lit match over a big mound of lighter fluid-soaked charcoal.

"Yes, what are you doing?" I could tell he didn't like having to ask twice.

"Well, ah, we're about ready to have a barbeque, officer."

"Not on this sidewalk you aren't," the policeman said as he approached. I whispered to Bill, who was loading the second grill with charcoal, to go inside and keep Paul busy. "Do not let him come out here." (If Paul came out onto the sidewalk, the situation would deteriorate very, very quickly.)

"So officer, what seems to be the problem?"

Patrolman McCarty, one of San Francisco's finest I was to learn, read through the six city code sections that applied directly to the situation, and then just summarized two others that had peripheral relevance. In addition to cooking on San Francisco sidewalks, it was also against the law to start fires of any kind on them, to serve food on them, even to form lines of people waiting to be served on them. Walking, I gathered, was pretty much the extent of what San Francisco sidewalks were to be used for.

"Officer, tell me, do you like bluegrass music?"

The First Annual Paul's Saloon BBQ and Bluegrass Blowout was hugely successful. We served 275 Cajun meals, Paul did the biggest bar in the history of the Saloon, bigger even than when Bill Monroe played there, and High Country was absolutely incredible—best I've ever heard them. It turned out that Patrolman McCarty was a Virginia boy and surely did like his bluegrass music. I told him about the band I was in, that we were going to play that night. He told me he was a dobro player and a singer but didn't get to play with folks much since he'd moved out from Norfolk.

We talked for a few minutes and then he said, "Well, I'll tell ya Rick. You can't be cookin' or servin' food out here on the sidewalk. I won't have a chance to get back by here before my shift ends in three hours," he paused and looked directly into my eyes, "so, you've been warned. You understand what I'm sayin'?"

"I think so," I said.

"Yeah, you understand. Now how's about after work I go by the house and pick up my axe. You reckon I could sit in a spell with the, ah, whadya call it, the Glass Menagerie?"

"GRASS Menagerie."

"Right, right. You reckon?"

"We'd be honored," I said.

"Okay then, I'll see you later. And no barbequing….I don't expect to see any of this stuff when I come back in three hours. We're on the honor system. You hear?"

"I hear."

We had three more Blowouts after that first year, each better than the one before. We stopped only because Paul called it quits and sold out to a corporation that wanted to open a fern bar at 2513 Chestnut. I've gone on to bigger events, even more dinners, but never, ever, anything like the First Annual Paul's Saloon BBQ and Bluegrass Blowout. Oh, and in 1995, the Santa Cruz Bluegrass Society let me cook for them at one of their campouts. Excellent meal.

No Experience Necessary
March 2009

We all want to be liked. It's in our human make up, in our genes. And I think if you had to identify a category of people by whom we'd all like to be liked, it would have to be in-laws. And more importantly, mothers-in-law and fathers-in-law. And for us men, MOST importantly fathers-in-law. There's sort of a primal imperative about being accepted by your woman's progenitor. I've had two fathers-in-law in my life, both of whom had not much use for me. It's been a life-long problem.

I saw this coming well before marrying age, however. My first real tip off was Carol Murray's father. George Murray was a big, burly red-faced Irishman who didn't like me and sure didn't trust me. (I mean, to be honest, I wouldn't have trusted me either. I was seventeen and I was crazy in love with his sixteen-year-old daughter.) Carol was, in my junior year of high school, pretty much the perfect girl friend. She was beautiful, I mean actually beautiful.

She had long blond hair parted down the middle early hippie style, blue eyes that had an 'I dare you' sparkle to them, and she was smart with a sense of humor much drier than you'd expect to find in a high school sophomore. Oh, and Carol went to a different high school than I did….a Catholic school in Oakland, which made her exotic as well as a knock out. (The plaid skirt, starched white shirt, knee high socks…the complete Bishop O'Dowd High look….was enough to make a seventeen year old go mad.)

Yes, in the winter of 1965 I was knee-deep in love and waist deep in physical attraction….okay, neck deep. And you can bet Carol's father could see that, could feel it in his bones, which made him all the more distrustful. But it was more than not trusting me with his little girl. It was clear that he just didn't like me, detested me even, and he went out of his way to let me know. When I'd pick Carol up for a date, he never spoke. Not a word. He'd just look up from his newspaper and glower menacingly. Come to think of it, I never saw the man when he wasn't reclined in his Barcalounger reading a newspaper and looking menacing.

Okay, so I never met the man, never shook hands with him, never looked him in the eye. So how could I tell Mr. Murray didn't like me….truly hated me? Read on.

Carol and I had been dating about three months. We'd talk every night on the phone, date on the weekends, sneak out occasionally on weeknights to rendezvous….we were a couple. Going steady. I eventually got over the father disapproval thing; as long as I could still see Carol it really wasn't a problem. Then, one night, it was in mid-May, I received a phone call at home around 8:00 p.m.

"This is George Murray. Is Rick around? Can I speak to him?"

My first thought was that I didn't know any George Murray. Then it struck me and my body went rigid. "Oh my God," I thought, "it's Carol's father."

"Mr., ah, Murray," I asked unsteadily, "Carol's father?"

"Yeah, that's right, Carol's dad." I realized I'd never even heard his voice before.

"Hi, ah, yes, Mr. Murray, this is Rick."

"Listen, you interested in making a little money?" His voice was flat, emotionless. Not menacing. Not anything.

"Ah, sure, what did you have in mind?" I managed to say.

"Well, I dispatch down here at the main Western Union office in Oakland, down on Telegraph. You know where that is?"

"Yeah," I replied, not having a clue where this was going.

"Well, it's like this see, you know Mothers' Day is next Sunday. Mothers' Day's always the busiest time of the year down here, and we're short handed. You want to come and deliver some telegrams? Pays twelve fifty an hour."

I was speechless. This man whom I assumed hated my guts was actually offering me a job! And at TWELVE DOLLARS AND FIFTY CENTS AN HOUR. That was huge in 1965.

"Ah, sure, ah, I'd love to deliver telegrams. I can do that? I don't need to be, like, trained or certified or….."

"You don't need nothin'", he growled impatiently. "You got a car, don't ya? That's all you need. You want to deliver telegrams, you get down to the office and we'll give you some to deliver. Twelve and a half an hour."

"When?" I asked.

"Right now!" he barked.

"Now? Tonight?"

There was a long silence.

"Look, you want to make a few bucks delivering telegrams, get down here now. If not, that's fine too. 12 Telegraph Avenue. The Western Union Office." And then Carol's father hung up.

It was a little under an hour from Hayward to downtown Oakland, which meant I could show up for work by a quarter past nine. Which didn't make sense to me. Who goes to work at nearly ten o'clock at night? It didn't make sense to my mother either, but by the time I was seventeen she'd pretty much given up on controlling my comings and goings. All she said was to be careful. Good advice, I'd soon find.

At nine-fifteen sharp I walked into the Western Union office on Telegraph Avenue….it was just north of where Telegraph splits off from Broadway…..smack in the middle of bustling downtown Oakland, a big city compared to Hayward. I went up to the counter.

"Hi," I said with a broad smile, "I'm Rick Cornish reporting for work." The old woman at the counter was sorting through some envelopes and ignored me. I waited.

"Hello," I finally said again.

"Can't you see I'm doing something here, dammit. Just hold your friggin' horses." Another three or four minutes went by.

"Okay," she looked up from her stack of telegrams, "now what is it you want?"

"Ah, I'm Rick Cornish. Mr. Murray asked me to come here to work tonight. He….."

"George ain't here. George goes home at five. You wanna see George, you come back tomorrow."

"But….."

Before I could speak, a short man who looked to be in his mid-thirties approached the counter. He was prematurely bald, dressed in gray trousers and a gray Western Union shirt and he looked angry and frustrated and impatient and deeply unhappy, all at the same time.

"You the kid Murray called?"

"Yeah, my name is….."

"Jeez, what the hell took you so long?" He motioned for me to come around the counter and follow him. The old woman had already gone back to sorting through a stack of telegrams.

Jesse, whom I would later learn was hated by Mr. Murray as much as, if not more than, me, took me into a back room piled high with bulging white canvas bags of telegrams. The bags had drawstrings at the opening and each was stenciled with PROPERTY OF WESTERN UNION.

"You done this before?"

"No, you I see date Mr. Murray's daughter and….."

"Oh, Jeez. Well, it don't matter. Okay, listen," and then Jesse did my 'new employee orientation' which lasted all of six minutes. It wasn't that Jesse was hurrying, it was just that there really wasn't much to say. You take a canvas bag full of telegrams, a clip board with several stapled pages of names, addresses and signature boxes and a "Locaide", (a one inch-thick spiral-bound book of Oakland street maps) and you go to one address after another delivering telegrams.

"Okay, now, this is what you gotta remember," Jesse said, looking directly into my eyes for the first time for emphasis, "this is what's important. You NEVER let one of these friggin' pieces (telegrams) out of your hands until it's signed for. NEVER. You go to an address, you knock or ring, nobody answers, you knock or ring again, nobody answers, you write right here in the 'comments' box, ND."

"ND?"

"Non-Deliverable."

I just looked at him and finally asked, "That's it?"

"That's it, man. You take the bag, the list and the Locaide and you go to every address on the list and deliver what you can deliver and bring the rest back here. Questions?"

"Yeah, one question. Well, like, it's nearly ten o'clock. So, how's this work? Isn't it kind of late to be knocking on people's doors?"

"No, kid," Jesse said, for the first time showing some emotion in his eyes, "this is the PERFECT time for a delivery. In fact, it's a little early. See, the idea is to get rid of these damned things." He held up a telegram. "And you can't get rid of a piece unless you hand it to somebody AFTER THEY'VE SIGNED FOR IT. So, the later you go, the better chance somebody's gonna be home to hand it to. You get me?"

And suddenly I recognized the emotion that was in the dingy little gray-shirted man's face. It was sympathy. Touching, really.... sympathy for a complete stranger, for me. That should have tipped me off but, again, I was only seventeen.

"Okay, now look." Jesse pointed to a big map of the city taped to the wall. "This is your delivery zone." He used his index finger to outline the area. "This is the run that old man Murray built for you before he left today."

"For me?" I asked.

"Yep."

"But how did he know I was even going to do this thing? I didn't speak with him on the phone 'til about an hour ago. He must have called me from home." Probably reclining on his Barcalounger, I thought.

"Jeez, I dunno," Jesse said, "he just said you'd be here." He was back to being impatient. "Anyway, you find yourself out of this zone right here," he said circling again with his finger, "and you'll know you're lost. Got it?"

"Yes, I've got it. But how about a phone number where I can reach you if…."

"There's no reason you'll need to call me, kid. Take the bag, take the list, take the Locaide and get rid of those telegrams….as many as you can. Oh, and you'll need a flashlight. I suppose you don't got a flashlight"

I told him I did have a flashlight in my car, but Jesse handed me one of those long, black, heavy police flashlights, the ones that double as billy clubs. It had 'Property of Western Union' written on it with yellow magic marker.

"Better take this one. And dammit, you bring this sucker back, you hear? Them's expensive and it'll come outta your pay if you lose it. Oh, one more thing. Fill out this form so we'll know where to send your check." The form consisted of a line for my name, my mailing address and my Social Security Number. That was it. That was my employment application. I stuffed the clip board, the Locaide and the flashlight into the white canvas bag, slung it over my shoulder and walked out into the main part of the office. As I reached the door where I'd come in, Jesse came out from the back room.

"Hey," he yelled, "one more thing, and this is important. You hand 'em the piece and then you split. Right away. DO NOT wait for them to open the envelope. You understand that? You hand 'em the piece and then you split."

Still at the counter sorting piles of telegrams, the old woman chuckled to herself.

To say that, at seventeen, I was a little naive would be like saying that investors in Nigerian business opportunities lack a certain amount of financial acumen. As I pulled out into the busy traffic on Telegraph Avenue in my little black Volkswagen I felt like my life was about to change…..like I was about to march toward some new plateau. I was going to make some REAL money tonight, I was going to impress my girlfriend's dad, and, best of all, I was finally out there, in the real world. In less than two hours I'd gone from doing school homework to becoming a Western Union Man. That the whole telegraph office thing seemed a little, well, informal; that my training for the job hadn't amounted to much more than being given instructions on how to feed the next door neighbor's cats while they were on vacation; that the qualifications for the job were limited to being Carol's boyfriend and having a car—none of that mattered to me as I bobbed and weaved through big city traffic. Like Jesse'd said, just get rid of the pieces, man. How complicated could it be?

My first delivery was on McClintock Way, just one block off East 14th Street, the major thoroughfare that connected Oakland with all the small cities and towns that line the eastern side of the San Francisco Bay. I knew how to get to East 14th, and finding McClintock wasn't hard. I parked my bug, grabbed the first of the telegrams, grabbed my clipboard and big black flashlight and headed to the wood frame apartment building across the street. And it was at that very moment…..that instant, midway across the little side street off East 14th Street ……that it hit me like a fist to my solar plexus. I was in West Oakland, notorious, dangerous West Oakland. In a neighborhood that was very poor and very run down and very…..black. All black, in fact.

It was after ten and the street was empty, no one in sight. I shined my flashlight on the apartment building and spotted #18. And a moment later there I was, my finger hovering over the doorbell button. I could hear a TV inside. 'Push the button. PUSH THE BUTTON!' I pushed the doorbell button and the apartment door immediately swung open.

"Mamma, it's Western Union," a little girl, of ten or so, said over her shoulder. Her mother appeared at the door, opened the screen, took the clip board out of my hand and with the pen dangling from a string tied to the clip board, she signed below her printed name. She handed the clip board back to me and held out her hand for her telegram. I gave it to her and she closed the door. Not a single word was exchanged between us.

Once back into the car, I locked both doors, slumped as far down into my seat as I could and sat for a while. For the first time since George Murray called me earlier in the evening, I took some time to think the whole thing through. I remembered back to the map on the wall that Jesse used to show me my delivery area; it was all West Oakland…..only West Oakland. I remembered that Jesse had told me George personally "built the run" just for me, his daughter's boyfriend. And I remembered seeing what looked like sympathy in Jesse's eyes when he showed me my zone. Then there was the flashlight, the baton, that Jesse insisted that I bring along.

BINGO! My girlfriend's father was trying to get me killed, or at least have the crap beat out of me. And he had the perfect alibi… he was sitting at home in his Barcalounger reading the paper. And if that didn't work out, he was going to prove to Carol I was nothing but a sniveling little wimp who high-tailed it back to my mama. It didn't take long to choose the latter scenario.

I started the VW, made a U-turn in the middle of the street, and drove back to East 14th. I headed south, toward Hayward and home, but only drove about two miles. I had to pee…..bad. I pulled into a Jack in the Box. There were five or six black guys in the parking lot. It looked like they were passing around a bong. Maybe I should keep going. No, I had to pee. NOW. When I stepped inside, every head turned toward me and the place went quiet. People actually stopped talking, like in a scene from a cowboy movie where the stranger walks into the saloon and the locals give him the once over. Except this was a Jack in the Box in the middle of West Oakland, the locals were all black and the stranger was me, a white boy wearing a surfer shirt, blue jeans and Converse tennis shoes. And the white boy had rubbery legs and fear written on his face, which had to be visible to the thirty or so customers in the place. I went straight to the restroom, did my business, and when I came back out……I was ignored. I was just another customer.

I went to the counter and bought a large Coke and two tacos.

'Dammit', I thought, getting back into my bug. 'DAMMIT! I'm gonna do this. I'll show that bastard.' It wasn't to prove anything to Carol. It wasn't for the money. It was for George Murray.

I'd left the Western Union office at about 10:00 p.m. with 125 pieces; I returned at 5:45 a.m. with 59.

"More than half." Jesse said after scanning my list. "That ain't bad, kid. I figured you'd a been back by midnight with a full bag. And all these ND's, you knocked and waited and knocked again, right? 'Cause if you didn't, Murray will know and he'll mop up the floor with ya. Where's the flashlight?"

"In the bag," I said.

Jesse looked me up and down.

"You want another run tonight?"

"Sure."

"Same route, you know."

"Sure," I repeated in not much more than a whisper. I was dead tired.

"You done okay, kid. Be back here at ten tonight." Jesse said.

I delivered Western Union telegrams in West Oakland for the next four nights, right up 'til Mothers' Day. (Didn't attend much school that week.) A week later, I got a fat check in the mail. Carol and I broke up a few months later, just before school ended in June. I started dating another girl at Bishop O'Dowd, Lindsay Parody. The following December, a week before Christmas, I got a call from Jesse, who wanted to know if I'd like a little work. I said sure.

In all I worked seven holidays delivering for Western Union until I went away to college. All of the deliveries were in West Oakland, (Jesse made sure I knew that it was George who always 'personally' built my routes.) I never delivered a telegram to a non-African American. What I learned over time was that virtually all of the pieces that I was given to be delivered were from Social Services. They either contained good news or bad news. (Hence Jesse's warning that first night to hand folks their envelope and then get the hell out of there.) Needless to say I never got a tip in three years (don't Western Union delivery guys always get tips in the movies?). But neither did I ever get attacked or harmed in any way. I was threatened many times, but that was mainly for waking people up at 3:00 AM. Mostly when people answered the door they did just what that first young mother had done. They signed and took their envelope and closed the door.

Cello's Map; A Cautionary Tale
August 2008

Since attending my first bluegrass festival in 1976 much of my life has been shaped by this traditional American art form. That said, I've worked very hard and been very careful not to allow my almost manic pursuit of traditional bluegrass, (listening to it, watching it performed, performing it myself, playing it with friends, building entire vacations around it and, eventually, working to preserve it through a non-profit organization), to interfere with the other parts of my life. I think family-wise I've done okay, (my wife, I'm sure, will have her own perspective on this), and with respect to my career I've been able to keep my avocation and my vocation pretty much separate. I say pretty much because once, twenty-five years ago, I allowed the two to get a little too close and the result was a near train wreck that could have destroyed, or at least severely damaged, my career.

In the early eighties the Grass Menagerie was arguably the least-known bluegrass act in all of Northern California. (We still hold that dubious distinction, but that's another story.) The band had only one goal at that time, and that was to play at Paul's Saloon. (For the uninitiated, Paul's was THE bluegrass venue on the West Coast for many years—everybody who was anybody on the national bluegrass scene played in that little hole in the wall in San Francisco's Marina District.) The band, Dave Guarante, Bill Schneiderman, Dave Woerner and I, practiced and we practiced and we practiced. And we sent an endless stream of demo cassettes and promo packages to San Francisco. What we lacked in raw talent we made up for in tenacity. Finally, after about a year of beating our heads against the wall, I received a phone call from the MAN, Paul Lampert. "You guys still want to play in my store (never understood why, but Paul always referred to his bar as 'the store')?" "Sure", I said holding my breath, "when?" "When do you think? (Expletive.) Tonight! (Expletive. Expletive.) Why the (expletive) do you think I called you?"

That night, a rainy Saturday night, the Grass Menagerie debuted at Paul's Saloon. We stood on the same tiny stage where Bill Monroe and Ralph Stanley and Jim and Jesse had stood. I can't remember exactly how we went over that first time, but we must have been okay, because a couple months later Paul called back. Bingo, we were in.

(Years later, after Paul had sold out and his "store" had become just another fern bar in the Marina, Lynn and I and Ed Neff, the legendary fiddler, and his wife, Brijjet, went sailing with him. As Paul and I stood alone steering the sixty-foot vessel underneath the San Francisco Bay Bridge, I finally had the chance to ask him a question that had been on my mind for a long, long time. "Do you remember that first time you called me, wanted us to play that very night? What was that all about?" "Oh,", he said without hesitation, "it was that little Alison what's-her-name… you know, the one who's such hot stuff nowadays. She called me the morning of their booking at the Saloon and tried to hold me up for more money. Wanted three hundred. Hell no, I said to her, I pay what I pay. If that isn't good enough, go find yourself a street corner." He laughed that insane, snarling laugh of his. "So when she and her husband backed out, you know, at the last minute, who else could I get with such short notice? Nobody any damn good would have taken it." (A belated 'thank you', Alison Kraus.)

But I digress. Back to the story at hand. After three years at Paul's, our quartet seemed about as stable as a Lutheran choir when, one rainy, stormy Saturday night at the Saloon, in walked a guy who would change everything. He looked more like a panhandler than a musician (turned out he was both at the time.) This scruffy, soaking wet guy walks in with his fiddle case, listens till our break and then strides up to me with a huge, intense and unembarrassed grin and asks if he can sit in. I ask him what tunes he does and he smiles. "I don't really play 'tunes'," he says, "I just sort of play. But it comes out okay. You'll see." I didn't like the sound of the guy's answer but there was something about him, something in his penetrating sky-blue eyes that seemed to hold me when he spoke. I said we'd maybe talk about it later and made no commitment.

By one-fifteen the place had pretty much emptied out and so I invited the stranger up on stage, much to the annoyance of the other three band members. To our collective surprise, he grabbed a chair on the way up, plopped it in the middle of the stage, sat down, put his fiddle between his legs as though it was a cello and said, "Let's do it, man." Well, we did it, and it was the kind of music I'd always known I would be a part of someday. His name was Cello, he was a street person, more or less, with a pregnant

French wife and above all, he was a brilliant fiddler. Gypsy violinist. Cajun fiddler. Classical musician. Down and dirty rocker. And of course a gifted bluegrass and old time fiddler. He was all of these things, and by the end of the evening, he was also a member of the Grass Menagerie.

The problem was, however, that Cello and his wife (I think they were married), Monique, had no transportation, which is to say, no car. And they lived forty-five miles to the north in the City. Cello had a simple plan; he and his pregnant wife would hitchhike down for gigs. I was skeptical.

"That's crazy," I told him, "totally undependable. We're standing on stage ready to start performing and you're still at a freeway entrance in San Francisco." Cello laughed and looked at me like I was a child and he was the adult explaining how things work.

"You ever hitch hike with a pregnant broad, man?" I hadn't, but I caught his point.

They were able to hitch a ride down to San Jose for the first gig Cello did with us, (it was just a week after we'd met him at Paul's), and afterward the two of them came home with me and slept in one of our guest rooms. And it was the very next morning that I veered slightly off the well beaten path and toward the train wreck ten years in the future. You see, Lynn and I had just moved into our new home up in the San Jose foothills and it was a damned big house. Two stories, four large bedrooms, huge family room, bigger living room, formal dining room, covered patio; just lots and lots of space. Way, way bigger than we needed. You see where this is going….the Grass Menagerie needed a fiddle player, one who lived in San Jose. Cello and Monique needed a roof over their head. There was the connection. It was simple, to me at least. My wife needed a little convincing. Okay, a lot of convincing, but in the end my crazy new band mate and his French wife were invited to move into one of our spare bedrooms. And they did.

Co-habitation actually went quite well. Lynn and I went to the office all day; Cello and Monique chilled at home, so they had the house to themselves. Each evening when we arrived home Monique had dinner ready….a live-in French chef! (Well, not every evening, but certainly when she felt like it….and when Lynn and I felt like eating vegetarian…..no, not Vegan.) Cello even did chores around the house. (I remember coming home one day and discovering that he'd drained my backyard's entire water feature--waterfall, stream, pond, everything, cleaned out the gunk and refilled it. Cello had a profound connection with my koi pond, though it had been years since that the raccoons had wiped out the fish. But that's another story.) The two of them contributed to groceries. And they were fun to have around. Lynn and I had become adults somewhere along the way…. professionals….. suburbanites…..home-owners and closing in on middle age. I'm not saying we were stick-in-the-muds by any means, but neither were we the free spirits of years gone by. Cello was the free spirit of all free spirits. A mad man who was as comfortable talking about Dostoyevsky, as he was bs'ing about college basketball. His beard, sparse and patchy, his hair slightly frizzed and mad scientist-like, and those crazy, crazy intense eyes of his. The kind of eyes Rasputin's musician kid brother would have had if Rasputin had had a musician kid brother. And Monique was so European. I remember the first night the four of us had dinner together; Lynn and I watched in rapt fascination as she ate every bite of food with both knife and fork in hand.

And the band! The band was playing better and better and more and more all the time. With a hot new fiddle player, one who not only played his fiddle like a Cello but was actually named Cello, gigs came pouring in. We began doing numbers that featured our new guy and the audiences ate it up. Musically, it was about the best time of my life up to that point and I was determined to keep our roll going as long as possible. Then two things happened within about a week of each other that caused me to veer off even further and aim dead on toward a full throttle freight train. First, Cello, who once bragged to me that he'd never in his life held down a steady job, put two and two together and realized that he needed more money than he could raise playing the fiddle if he was going to support a wife AND a baby. He was a free spirit, a gypsy, an eccentric. But he was also about to become a father.

Second, I received a call from my counterpart in the County Planning Department letting me know that it was time for the official map of school district boundaries in Santa Clara County to be updated. Let me back up a little. I worked for the County Superintendent of Schools, I was the Director of Planning, and as such, it was my group that was responsible for maintaining accurate and up-to-date large-scale maps, as well as narrative descriptions, of the boundaries of school districts in our jurisdiction. These were THE legal designations of boundary lines; they were used by the Assessor's Office for determining tax bills, by the Registrar of Voters for determining to whom to send ballot measures, and so on. This was obviously a very, very serious function of our department and we took it very, very seriously. When territory swaps were made between school districts we'd change the maps accordingly. When new streets or new sub divisions were developed, one of my staff would do the necessary research, feed the information to a cartographer with whom we contracted, and the maps, as well as the written legal descriptions, would be updated.

But the County Planning Director was calling me about something else. Every ten years or so a smaller scale map, the fold up sort like you get from Triple A, was produced showing school district boundaries. These were distributed, free of charge, to a variety of governmental agencies, to businesses like real estate offices and to the public at large. You see, in what school district a particular piece of property is located can be extraordinarily important for any number of reasons. I'd not been around when the old map was done, but I learned I was responsible for creating a new school district boundary map that reflected all of the changes that had taken place over the course of the past nine years.

Even before our telephone conversation ended my brain had made the bluegrass connection. It was a natural. I couldn't use our regular cartographer to update the old map; it would have cost us a fortune and I didn't even have a budget. And we most definitely didn't need someone at that level. We needed a person, any person, with decent drafting skills who was smart enough to look at lines on many large scale maps, one at a time, and, using cartographic tape, place them on a smaller scale map. And who did I know who was smart enough to do that? Only the fiddle player in my band who: 1) needed to stick around San Jose so he could keep playing in my bluegrass band; 2) needed a job desperately; and 3) was smart enough to attend Princeton. (And Cello really did attend Princeton. He was there, living in a dorm, until he got booted out. His freshman year.) I realize I've left this out of my story. Sorry. In addition to being an unnaturally, almost supernaturally gifted fiddle player, Cello was a genius. As in 166

IQ. Crazy, most definitely, but a genius too. That same day, a job was offered and a job was accepted.

Cello took to the project like a fish to water, a cat to cat nip, a stoned hippie to a hookah. We'd initially estimated that the entire project, from start to delivery to the printer, would take five months, but by the end of thirty days we realized it would be done a lot sooner, maybe within three months, three and a half max. Cello would sit at the big drafting table near the rear of the department and just sort of go into a trance. It was the same concentration I saw when he played music. I naturally had one of my senior guys supervise him very closely at first, but there was really no worry. He was addicted to detail…..to accuracy. And his work ethic, oh man his work ethic. This was the guy who'd bragged about never having an eight to five, and here he was taking two ten minute smoking brakes and a half hour for lunch to eat the cheese and tofu sandwiches Monique would send along with him to work. And sometimes he'd stay after five just because he didn't want to stop in the middle of a new sub-division. It was amazing. He was all I could have asked for.

We were paying Cello pretty well. In one month he'd bought an old clunker, a pea-green Nisan which he and Monique name 'mon petit pois". The next month he and Monique moved into their own apartment. (I co-signed for the PG and E.) Monique was getting big; the two seemed happy. The wanderlust that had seemed to grip Cello so when we'd first met that rainy night at Paul's Saloon seemed to be losing its grasp. He was still Crazy Cello, still nowhere near being like anyone I'd ever met before, but there was a change. Lynn and I attributed it to the baby. Cello was going to be a dad.

Our temporary draftsperson finished the school district boundary map in three months to the day. We proofed it, proofed it again, shipped it off to our cartographer and paid him an arm and a leg to look it over, and then we delivered it to the printer. As the project was finishing up I'd already begun looking around for more work to offer Cello; he was a good, smart, hard worker, someone worth keeping around. At first Cello seemed interested in a new project, but then, the weekend after the map was finished, he came to see me. I remember it so well. I was working in my shop, using my router to make a house number plaque to replace the old, funky one, when he came walking up the driveway. The moment I saw his face I knew why he was there.

"Hey, man, I got somethin' to tell you."

"Yeah, I know." I turned off the bluegrass music that was blaring in competition with the router and looked into those dancing sky blue eyes of his.

"You guys been good to me. Good to US, me and Monique. But I gotta get movin'. Man, I GOTTA get movin'. Rick-man, I've never stayed in one place this long since I was a kid at home with my family. You know what I'm sayin'? It's like, ah, gettin' existential. You know?"

I nodded and after a long moment, I asked, "Where are you going?"

"We don't know. And dig it, man, that's what's cool about getting' goin'. That we don't know." Cello and I hugged a big, long bear hug and he turned and walked away and I never saw him again. I remember that brief meeting very, very well.

And I also remember very well my first conversation with Janice Brown nine years later, in the spring of 1994. (I'm using a fictitious name here for reasons that will soon become clear.) I was in my office and my secretary poked her head through the door.

"I've got a Ms. Brown. Something about a district boundary. I told her Larry handles boundaries, but she said she wanted to talk to the Director. Okay?"

"Sure," I said, "put her through."

"Hello Rick. Janice Brown here. I've got what I'm assuming will be a simple matter, but we really do need to get the ball rolling. You see, XYZ Unified School District (again a fictitious name) is under the mistaken impression that the property my husband and I have purchased four our new home does not fall within their boundaries. I need you to call the district people, preferably the superintendent, and explain that they're mistaken. Could you make the call this afternoon? My husband and I are very eager to get this cleared up."

"Mrs. Brown, what makes……"

"Please, call me Janice."

"Alright. Janice, what leads you to believe that XYZ has made a mistake about its boundaries?"

"The map."

"What map?"

"Your map."

"My map?"

"Yes, your map. Santa Clara County School District Boundary Map, produced by the Center for Educational Planning, Santa Clara County Office of Education, May, 1985. You're familiar with this map, are you not?"

"Yes, yes, of course I am," I said. "Mrs. Brown….er…..Janice, let me get your telephone number and I'll……."

"Don't you need the property's parcel number? Surely you must need the parcel number."

"Oh, oh, yes, absolutely. Please, give me the parcel number. We'll definitely need that." I dutifully wrote down the parcel number and Mrs. Brown's phone number and promised I'd get back to her later that afternoon, once we had a chance to research the discrepancy. But in my heart of hearts I already knew what the problem was. As I hung up the phone and closed my eyes I had an absolutely perfect, detailed, Technicolor image of Cello in my mind. It wasn't a picture of Cello sitting at the big drafting table, or of Cello and Monique in the tiny new apartment they'd rented, or of them sitting proudly in their beloved Petit Pois. No, the image I had in my head was of Cello walking in out of the rain into Paul's Saloon, his wild hair and scraggly beard dripping wet, his fiddle case tucked tightly under his arm, his sky blue eyes wild and fierce.

The sick feeling I had in my stomach only worsened when Larry Shirey, our school district organization guy, and I sat down to review his hastily done research an hour later.

"This was an easy one to spot." He pointed to a little yellow area, about a quarter the size of a pencil eraser, at the upper right of the map spread out on my conference table. "There, you see? That's the Brown's parcel, about four acres. See how it's colored in in yellow. Should be blue. And the boundary line should be here….. not there." His finger moved less than a quarter of an inch.

"You're sure," I asked?

"Yep, we've checked both the 500 scale map and the written legal description. What we've got is a mistake, a tiny, itsy-bitsy one, on our fold up." 'Fold up' is what we called the small scale map we gave out to the public….the map my band mate, fresh off the mean streets of San Francisco, had created nine years earlier.

"When you think about it," Larry said, "it's really a very, very small glitch. At this scale map, the boundary line itself is one hundred, maybe one hundred and fifty feet thick. We've found bigger mistakes than this on the fold up. It's to be expected. We just haven't found one until today that somebody's based a $1,700,000 property purchase on."

"ONE POINT SEVEN MILLION? JUST FOR THE LAND?"

"Yep," Larry said with an ironic grin. "Can you imagine somebody going out and dropping nearly two million bucks on a piece of land without checking first to see what school district it was in. One simple call is all it would have taken. Instead they use a

1000-scale map. That's not what this map is for. We tell people that all the time, but you know, people just don't listen. People care about what school district they're in, but they don't listen."

Yes, if there was one thing I knew after nearly twenty years in the business it was that folks, at least some folks, cared very, very much about what school district they lived in. Many cared because they knew, or believed they knew, that there was a wide disparity among districts in terms of quality of program, staff, facilities, etc. They certainly knew that there was a wide disparity in test scores. Others, mainly developers, knew how dramatically property values could vary from district to district, even neighboring districts. A house in school district A could be worth $300,000; if it were a block away, bringing it into school district B, it could be worth $700,000. Oh yes, people cared all right.

I kept my word and called Mrs. Brown back in the late afternoon, just before 5:00. I explained that the map she and her husband had included a small mistake, that parcel did not, in fact, lie in XYZ Unified School District, that the 1000-scale fold up map was not intended for precise designations of boundary lines, and that we were terribly sorry for the mistake. When I finished there was a very long silence and then a simple, polite, "Thank you, Mr. Cornish. We will be getting back to you." And with those eleven words began a chapter in my life which, though thankfully brief, was among my darkest.

Not surprisingly, given the stakes involved, it was not Mr. or Mrs. Brown who got back to us, it was their legal counsel. During a fairly brief telephone conversation the attorney filled me in on the details:

--Mr. and Mrs. Brown were both attorneys—obviously quite bright and well to do and certainly not fools, as in people who represent themselves in a court of law. Their specialty, both their specialties, was tort law;

--The couple was from out of county and had purchased the four-acre piece of property where they would build their dream home, permits for which had already been issued, and where they would raise their children, none of whom had yet been born.

--The real estate agent who sold the parcel to the Browns assured them that it lay easily within XYZ School District, which, according to a study that had appeared, quite truncated of course, in Newsweek Magazine earlier that spring, was the 48th best school district in the United States. The agent 'proved' the lot was in XYZ by showing the Browns the 'Santa Clara County School District Boundary Map, produced by the Center for Educational Planning, Santa Clara County Office of Education, May, 1995.'

--Mr. and Mrs. Brown would, we were promised, pursue this matter with every fiber of their beings.

Here's what I knew in 1994, after spending close to twenty years in public service: 1) anybody can sue anybody for anything; 2) a jury can find for a plaintiff, and that finding can stick regardless of statute, case law or evidence; 3) in a civil suit, money talks. Now, nearly fifteen years later, I believe that the same is true, only double.

But to be totally honest, I wasn't really all that worried about what a judge or jury would decide. When we published the fold up map we were sure to include on both sides a statement that read: "This map has been prepared to provide a broad overview of the locations of school districts, school district offices and individual schools in Santa Clara County. For precise information about school district boundaries and the exact location of addresses within education agencies in the County, please contact the Center for Educational Planning at 408-468-5912." Sure, a jury could disregard the disclaimer and find for the Browns, but it didn't seem likely.

No, what was worrying me was far, far more personally calamitous. That same night after speaking with the Brown's attorney I was stricken with what's called 'situational insomnia", and for nearly a year thereafter I went to sleep, (or tried going to sleep) playing and re-playing some variation of the following mental tape:

Plaintiff's Counsel: Mr. Cornish, what is the full name of the person who actually created the map in question?

Defendant: Cello.

Plaintiff's Counsel: Full name please.

Defendant: Cello, that's it. Just Cello, that's how I knew him.

Plaintiff's Counsel: Could you describe how you and Mr. Cello first met?

Defendant: Well, I, ah, met him in a bar.

Plaintiff's Counsel: Can you tell the jury what training Mr. Cello had in cartography?

Defendant: Well, I know that he was admitted to Princeton.

Plaintiff's Counsel: To study cartography?

Defendant: No, to study music, with a minor in world religions.

Plaintiff's Counsel: In what year did he graduate from Princeton?

Defendant: He didn't, he flunked out his freshman year. First semester.

Plaintiff's Counsel: Can you tell us what experience Mr. Cello had in map making?

Defendant: Well, he was very good with his hands. He was a gifted fiddler....er, ah, violinist.

Plaintiff's Counsel: In the symphony?

Defendant: No, in my bluegrass band. The Grass Menagerie.

Plaintiff's Counsel: The Glass Menagerie?

Defendant: The GRASS Menagerie.

Plaintiff's Counsel: Where was Mr. Cello living at the time he was hired by the Center for Educational Planning?

Defendant: He and his wife lived with my wife and me. In one of our spare bedrooms.

Plaintiff's Counsel: Where had they lived before that?

Defendant: On the streets…..in San Francisco.

And so on into the early hours of the morning. Night after night I would replay the cross-examination in my mind, each time refining it, plugging any escape routes I was naïve enough to imagine might be there for me. It was like a bad dream, a nightmare, but it wasn't a dream. Mr. and Mrs. Brown were real, their attorney was real, and the 1.7 million they'd spent on a rocky hillside in a sub-par school district, just a few hundred feet away from the nation's 48th best district…..that was real.

I didn't tell my wife. I didn't tell my boss, who was the County Superintendent of Schools. I didn't tell a single one of my friends. I didn't even share much with my staff…they just knew the 'Browns thing' was an issue that was hanging, (one that seemed to make the boss jumpy).

We never heard from the Browns' attorney again. Never heard from the Browns. A couple of times Larry asked me if I'd like him to quietly nose around and see what he could find out, but both times I said no. Let the shoe drop when it will drop. We knew these things took time. Sometimes a long, long time. We'd wait.

In treatment, once your body is rid of all cancerous cells, you are said to be in 'remission'. Five years of being cancer free wins your condition the new title of 'CURED'. I gave myself two years of being contact-free before I finally decided my world was not going to crumble around me. Twenty-four months. A long, lonely period in my life.

Would I have lost my job if the truth had come out about my hiring crazy Cello off the streets to prepare an official, county government-produced map? I'm guessing probably not. But I have no doubt that serious and long-term damage would have been done to my career in public service had the truth about the hiring come out in either court or in a deposition. I was very lucky. And I learned an important lesson. As important as bluegrass music is, it's a distant second to being able to provide for your family.

Plan C
February 2004

I love most animals—my Lab Alex and my Border Collie Sid are at the top of the list. There are a few animals that just sort of creep me out (snakes for example), even fewer that I don't like (parrots for example), but there's only one kind of animal that I can honestly say I hate. And that's a raccoon. We have a saying around Whiskey Creek, which is what we call our ten acre plot of ground up here in the Gold Country)—the only good coon's a dead coon. Of course, I've never actually killed one, but that's not for lack of trying.

In 1991 I spent the entire summer building a waterfall and pond in my back yard at our home in the East San Jose foothills. Water came tumbling down the hillside, collecting in four little pools along the way, and then finally splashed into a large, irregularly shaped pond. Once the stream, waterfall and pond were completed, I spent the remainder of the summer landscaping the area with lush, tropical plants…tree ferns, rubber plants, philodendra, palms.

It was beautiful. So much so, in fact, that Lynn and I decided that at summer's end we'd throw a big party to sort of christen the new back yard and its spectacular water works. My wife suggested that we buy a few gold fish to put in the pond, but I had an even better idea. "Let's ask that everyone who comes to the party bring a live fish to put into the pond," I said, "it'll be fun."

Over one hundred people came to our Picking Party-Pond Dedication-BBQ, a good half of them bluegrass pickers. What a glorious day of music and food and friends. And we netted a BUNCH OF fish, and all but one was alive. There were minnows, big gold fish, little gold fish, bottom feeders, koi….you name it, somebody brought one or two. The morning after the bash I went out and did a head count—sixty-eight in all. And they seemed right at home.

The next week Lynn bought a book on the care and feeding of pond fish, we bought just the right kind of food for our new pets, I bought a new water filter and kept the pond clean and the sixty-eight fish thrived. We even began naming some of the bigger ones. One of the koi was named Sal because he was exactly the color of a leaf of Romaine lettuce. My wife named one of the little catfish Doc after Doc Watson. And of course her favorite goldfish, Whitey, whom she'd had for years and kept in a goldfish bowl, got to join his new fish friends.

As summer faded into fall and then fall into winter, the fish seemed happy and healthy. Every now and then I'd try counting them, just to make sure they were all okay, all still present and accounted for. We were even beginning to think that maybe in the spring we'd hear the patter of little fin steps in the pond.

And then one morning--it was the 17th of February 1992--Lynn went out to feed the fish and a moment latter I heard a scream. "What's wrong," I yelled, running out to the pond. Lynn just stood there shaking her head. All of the water lilies that had floated in the pond were strewn on the ground. Little fish skeletons littered the ground and floated in the water. On the red brick patio bordering the pond, there was a clutter of little footprints. Actually, they looked more like little handprints. Raccoons.

We frantically checked to see if any fish were left alive. There were thirteen swimming at the bottom, and they included Whitey, Doc and Sal. I fetched a washtub and, using a smaller bucket bailed enough pond water to fill the tub two-thirds full. Then Lynn carefully caught each of the survivors with a nylon net and placed them in the tub. Together we carried the tub into the garage and pulled the door closed tight. I was flying out of town the next day and would be gone three days. Figuring out what would have to be done about the fish would have to wait till the weekend. They'd be okay in the shop for a few days.

One of the first things I did when I returned home Friday evening was to go out and check the fish. All thirteen were right where I'd left them, swimming around. (I noticed they were as close to the bottom as possible.) That night Lynn and I agreed on a strategy, at least to get us through the winter months. I'd go out the next morning and buy some chicken wire, stretch it over a wooden frame and we'd figure out a way to secure it over the pond. Then, in the spring, we'd come up with a more permanent, more esthetic solution.

The next morning as I was leaving for Orchard Supply Hardware, I glanced over at the garage on my way to the driveway and noticed that the door was slightly ajar. I rushed over, pulled open the door and there on the concrete floor I saw a familiar scene….little pieces of fish, mostly heads and skeletons and, of course, little muddy hand prints. I looked in the tub hoping against hope to see Doc and Sal, and Whitey the goldfish. There were only more lifeless fish parts.

Up until that Saturday morning in February of '92 I guess I never really had any feelings about raccoons, one way or another. I mean, I'd owned a Davey Crockett hat when I was eight, I'd seen families of raccoons occasionally while camping and I suppose somewhere in the back of my mind I was aware that they could be pests. Then, when we'd discovered what they had done to the fish in the pond, I was perfectly clear on their peskiness. But now, standing in the garage, looking down on what was left of the last 13 fish, the survivors, things had changed. They were no longer pests, they were enemies, and I hated them. It was as if those fish had trusted me with their lives, had known they wouldn't have a chance in the tub, but also had known I would keep them safe. I'd let them down. The night before I hadn't closed the garage door quite shut. I couldn't do anything about the 68 fish, about Doc and Sal and Whitey, but I could, and would, do something about the raccoons.

Initially I hadn't planned on killing them. I would rent a live-catch trap (a wire cage sort of affair with a triggering mechanism and a door that sprang shut), bait it and, one by one, I'd catch the coons and haul them far, far away from my neighborhood out into the country—they deserved worse, but I was not a vengeful man….. not at that point. So, instead of going to Orchard Supply to buy chicken wire that morning, I went to Hecker's Feed and Farm Supply on Alum Rock Avenue. An old wood frame structure wedged between Pep Boys and Jeanne's Quick Cuts and Tanning Salon, Hecker's seemed out of place there on Alum Rock. It was from another time, when people changed their own oil and got honest tans doing honest work in the sun.

"You say you want to rent a trap, not buy one, and you got yourself a whole family 'a coons," old Mrs. Hecker asked from behind the counter.

"Right."

"Okay, but this could end up costin' you a lot more money than just buyin' a trap."

"Why's that," I asked impatiently.

"Coons is smart," she said squinting her eyes, "they's a lot smarter than you might give 'em credit for. It's gonna take a while to catch just one, and sounds like you got yourself four, maybe five. Gonna take a while to catch that many coons."

"So how much to buy a trap?" I asked steeling myself for the bad news.

The old woman looked me over, still squinting. "Sixty-five. But it's a good one. You get a coon in there and he ain't gonna get out."

"So you think this'll do the trick, huh?" I asked, wanting her to convince me to spend the sixty-five bucks.

"No sir," she said without hesitation, "no, I don't think it'll do the trick one bit. I think if you buy this cage and take it home and put some bait in it, and keep removing the old, stale bait and putting fresh bait in, night after night, in a couple a weeks you'll get tired of having to tend to it and you'll lose interest and that'll be that. That's what I think."

I took out my Visa card and handed it to her.

"Well," I said, "you're wrong about that. I've got a score to settle with these raccoons." The old woman chuckled at that.

Mrs. Hecker of Hecker Feed and Farm Supplies was dead wrong. It took well over three weeks before I gave up. Like the ultimately doomed slot machine player, my interest was kept alive for a while because a few times the bait had actually been removed without setting off the trigger. And once the bait was gone and the spring-loaded door was shut….mysteriously with no raccoon inside. It was like getting nibbles but never quite hooking the fish. So, less than a month after the terrible "seafood buffet" as we'd come to call it, the live-catch trap was stowed in the garage rafters. I'd had enough.

But it turned out the raccoons hadn't. In the five or six years that Lynn and I had lived in our hillside home on Chula Vista, we'd never even seen a raccoon, despite the fact that we lived less than half a mile from a sprawling and quite wild county park of several hundred acres. But all that changed in February of 1992. It's like we'd suddenly been discovered by the locals. It took several months after our September fish party for our backyard to become noticed, but once it had, it became a preferred destination for the raccoon population. They would come in groups of two or three, usually late at night, looking for food and water and who knows what else. Lynn fed our three cats out on the deck, so the dried cat food became a target. When we caught on to that and moved the cat bowls into the laundry room where we fed our two dogs, the coons started coming into the house through the doggie door, the dog food proving to be a bonus they hadn't counted on. Sure, we began closing the doggie door at night but, forget one night, and the raccoons would be back in. Our dogs, who slept upstairs with us, would occasionally hear the intruders and make a racket, but all that did was interrupt our sleep. By the time I got downstairs, they'd be gone. And what if they hadn't? What was I going to do with a cornered raccoon? These animals, I was learning, have quite a nasty reputation.

The coons were a nuisance to be sure, and a couple of times I considered getting the trap down from the rafters, but, as my departed mother used to say, "folks can get used to anything." Which is what happened. And besides, there were periods of several months at a time when we wouldn't see a single raccoon. But then, in the spring of 1996, something happened that shattered the uneasy cold war between the humans and the coons. In the early morning hours, Alex, our blond lab, had gone downstairs, out the doggie door and into the back yard to empty his bladder and had inadvertently come upon a big nasty male raccoon. Without even realizing it, much less trying, Al had cornered the animal and instinctively the two went at it. They made a terrible commotion and I went tearing downstairs and out the door just in time to see the coon skulking away. Alex stood in the shadows and seemed okay, but when I called him over to me, I saw he was bleeding from his stomach and his neck. And I that the coon had left a trail of blood. It was time for Plan B.

Surprisingly, old Mrs. Hecker remembered me when I stopped into Hecker's Feed and Farm Supply on the way home from work the next day.

"A box of 22 shorts," I said putting a ten-dollar bill on the counter.

"Still got yer coon problem, eh?" She squinted at me.

I nodded but didn't speak. I resented just a bit that Mrs. Hecker had been so right about the trap three years before.

"Ever shot a coon before," she asked as she rang up the box of bullets.

"Nope."

"They die hard, those coons….awful hard. And they's mean when they're cornered and meaner still when they're hurtin'. You got a good, reliable rifle?"

"Well," I said, "I've got a rifle." The truth is, I didn't really know anything about the ancient twenty-two I'd kept stored up in the rafters of the garage since my dad had died ten years earlier and left it to me. (Actually, I had a second gun, a snub nose that my Uncle Red had given me, but there was no way I was going to use that one. It creeped me out.)

"You'd best take care, young fella," Mrs. Hecker cautioned. "You'd best take that gun of yours out and fire it off some. Git to know it…..git to know it good 'a 'nuff so as when you shoot the coon, you shoot 'em dead."

"Give me two boxes of shorts instead of one," I said.

"Did ya say longs?" the old woman asked. Longs were, of course, longer, contained more gun powder and hence were more powerful.

"Yes," I said, "longs."

It turned out the twenty-two worked just fine. I took it to a firing range and squeezed off a whole box full of rounds. And it turned out, too, that I wasn't a half bad marksman….mid-way through the session, I actually started hitting the cardboard target, and even placed a few slugs within the outer concentric circles. No, I didn't cotton to guns but, dammit, forced to use one, I now knew I could.

It's difficult to convey the totality of my wife's objection to Plan B. It was vehement, it was haranguing, it was pretty much non-stop for the better part of a week. And then Lynn just gave up. We'd been together long enough for her to know when it was just no use. But she was able to extract a promise from me—I would not kill anything, or try to kill anything, in her presence. This meant that any raccoon stalking would have to take place after Lynn went upstairs to bed, which was actually okay since the coons didn't much come around till we'd retired anyway. The set up was pretty much perfect for coon hunting. I sat in the family room, in an overstuffed chair, my rifle at my side, facing the open double French doors that entered out onto the patio. I made sure a nice, big metal bowl of fresh cat food sat on the deck….it wasn't more than ten feet away from me. I would aim for the head and dispatch the animal with a single shot. Two if need be.

The first night I sat for two hours there in the dark and saw no raccoons. The second night, still no sightings. The third night I fell asleep just fifteen minutes into my vigil, and when I woke up an hour later, some of the cat food was gone. But who ate it? Coon or cat? It was a week before I finally saw my first raccoon. I'd dozed off, and when I awoke, there it was, on the counter nibbling the cat food. I reached for the rifle but before my fingers even touched the gun, the animal had disappeared into the night. 'Coons is smart,' Mrs. Hecker had said, 'they's a long sight smarter than you might give 'em credit for.' Right again.

I was considerably more tenacious with Plan B than I had with Plan A. By mid-summer, I'd had maybe ten coon sightings and, of them, only two resulted in shots being fired. In both cases I'd fired at retreating raccoons—and in both cases I'd missed. In July we had a heat spell, with five days of one hundred plus temperatures. One night I sat up for three hours waiting for a raccoon to come. It was so hot I knew I wouldn't be able to sleep anyway. Finally I gave up and went to bed but the moment my head hit the pillow, I remembered I'd left the twenty-two leaning against the couch in the family room….wouldn't do for Lynn to find it there the next morning. I went back downstairs to stow the rifle, picked it up and discovered I'd also forgotten to close the French doors. As I stepped toward the sliding doors, there before me on the patio, not four feet away, was a huge raccoon sitting on the brick floor daintily nibbling a bit of cat food. He sat frozen, caught in the darkness. I don't know who was more surprised. My heart thumped as I drew the cold steel of the twenty-two up to my cheek. In an instant I took aim and squeezed the trigger at nearly point blank range. Click. Not bang. Click. Mis-fire.

The raccoon looked up, directly into my eyes. It just stared, and I stared back for what seemed like a long time. And then very slowly, it stood up, turned and walked away. The coon didn't run. It walked.

The next morning I emptied the twenty-two rifle of its bullets, wrapped it up in an old flannel sheet and placed it up in the garage rafters, next to the live-catch trap. While not a superstitious man, I'm a firm believer in fate, and, for me, the misfiring of that rifle at point blank range was no chance occurrence. Lynn was delighted. She kept the dogs in at night. She made sure the doggie door was closed each night. We lived with the raccoons.

In 1999 I hired a young Vietnamese man named Charles Doan as a designer and web applications developer. I remember so well his first interview. I liked him right off but I was concerned about whether he'd stay with our group or just use the position as a stepping-stone—we were in the midst of the dot-com explosion.

"One final question, Charles. Why do you want this job? Why would you choose to work for a public agency with so many better paying positions out there?"

"Chiclets," he said with a mischievous grin.

"Chiclets?" I was certain I hadn't heard him correctly.

"You see, Mr. Cornish," he began slowly, "when I was a little boy in Vietnam I spent much time with American GI's. They liked me and figure I bring them good luck, and some times they would take me out with them on patrol. As a little boy I remember so many times I watch them eat their field rations. And when they finish, they always find a little white plastic-wrapped Chicklet, you know, a piece of gum, at the bottom of their ration pack. That just impressed me so, so much. Their government took good care of them, feed them, and even made sure that at end of meal, they could chew a piece of gum. I say to myself, one day I will work for that government. That has been my dream. That is why I am here."

I hired Charles on the spot, and in the months and years that followed, I was thankful I did. He and I became instant friends. Most days we took our lunches together. We would sit and swap stories and philosophize and generally laugh a lot. Charles was a bit of a player. He was not a young, innocent naïve Vietnamese immigrant…he knew his way around, could scam if he needed to, but he never scammed me, nor I him. Charles Doan knew San Jose's Southeast Asian community well. He knew the side visible to 'whites', as he called us, but he also knew the underbelly. He often bragged that he could find anything on the black market. "You tell me what you need, boss, I get it for you. Half price."

One day Charles and I sat in one of our favorite café's in "Little Saigon" having grilled lemon grass chicken and jasmine rice.

"You know the tropical fish store next door," my friend said, "it belong to my friend's uncle. Many interesting fish in friend's uncle's store….many legal, some not so legal."

"What do you mean," I asked.

"I mean this guy, Tran, he sell fish in there that are not suppose to be sold. You know? Forbidden by law. Fish and Game Department forbidden."

"Like?"

"Like some kind shark. Poison octopus. Stinger ray. Piranha from South America. You know about piranha, boss? They so ferocious, most ferocious of all fish….of all animals. I read that."

That afternoon Charles sent me an e-mail with a link to a web site about South American piranhas. "Friend's uncle sell this kind," the e-mail said. I clicked on the link…..

"Piranhas can be such effective eating machines because they have numerous upper and lower teeth that are short, triangular, and sharp. The teeth interlock and the jaws are extremely powerful, allowing these fish to chew continuously and to remove flesh in clean bites. The presence of blood is generally thought to be a stimulant to a feeding frenzy of flesh-eating piranhas. However, there is ample evidence to indicate that these fish are triggered into attacking behavior by frenzied and panic-like activity of victims."

I replied to Charles' e-mail—"And you say your friend's uncle can get these fish?"

A moment later, his response—"Yes, boss."

And it was there, sitting in front of my computer, alone in the quiet of my office, that Plan C was born.

There was much, much more work that would go into implementing the third and final plan. The pond built several years before was totally inadequate for piranhas. Through Internet research I came up with a design that both met the living requirements of the fish and my and Lynn's own esthetic requirements. I would build a large, redwood tank up against the thick concrete retaining wall at the foot of the hill in our back yard. Like the original pond, the tank would be the recipient of perpetually falling fresh water from a stone waterfall. But unlike the pond, the tank would have straight lines for better underwater maneuverability, and it would be deep, affording the fish a quick get away if need be. It took me two months and one thousand dollars to build the new tank-pond-waterfall. My friend Charles helped. Lynn was ambivalent about the new project. She didn't understand why we needed a second pond, but at least I'd let go of the "raccoon thing".

When the construction was finally complete and Charles and I filled the tank up with water and turned on the pump to activate the waterfall, it was a thing of beauty. Now there was just one more detail before bringing home our new pets.

"Hello," Mrs. Hecker said absentmindedly looking up from her feed catalogue. "Oh, it's you. The fella with the coon problem. Still got yer problem?" The old woman squinted at me, as though trying to read my mind, to anticipate what I was going to try next.

"Yes, mam, it's me. But I don't have a raccoon problem anymore. Getting along just fine with the raccoons. Like members of the family. But I do need to buy something raccoon-related. What kind of wire mesh do you have that a coon couldn't possibly chew through."?

"Wouldn't trust chicken wire, not if ya got somethin' valuable to protect from them nasty things. Whatcha trying to protect from the coons, Mr.?"

"Two expensive fish. A mated pair. Very rare."

Old Mrs. Hecker studied me a while before asking, "Rare eh? What kinda fish you say they were?"

"I didn't," was my only reply.

Mrs. Hecker sent me home with a panel of heavy-gauge, one-by-one galvanized fencing. When I pulled up into the driveway, I off loaded the panel, threw a plastic bucket into the cab and went inside to call Charles at home. "We're on for tomorrow," I said. "Okay, boss, on for tomorrow. Bring bucket."

After work the next day I followed Charles the two miles or so to the Asian Pacific Center, a huge shopping complex in the middle of Silicon Valley's most densely populated Asian community. Charles parked a good fifty yards from the Tran's Tropical Fish Store and motioned me to park next to his car. We'd already agreed that I would wait there in the truck. I handed him the white plastic bucket. Thomas was inside a long time and I began to wonder if something had gone wrong. Don't be ridiculous, I thought to myself, it's not like we're robbing a bank. It's not a federal offense, for God's sake.

Finally I saw him walking across the parking lot towards our vehicles. I started to get out but he shook his head. Thomas put the bucket into his trunk and pulled out of the shopping complex parking lot with me following. He drove about a mile, turned onto a residential street and then we both rolled to a stop and parked.

"They're beauties," he smiled broadly, "the very best I've ever seen."

"Charles, you've never seen a piranha in your life, what are you talking about?"

"Well, yes, that's true. But they are beauties."

I pulled out my wallet. "What do I owe you?"

"Nothing," he said. "My gift to you?"

"No, I can't let you do that. Those things were expensive."

"Can't take your money, boss. Gave my word to Tran. Told him I would not sell piranhas. He very cautious about who he give unlawful fish to. Federal law, you know."

"Federal?"

"Yes, boss, federal."

"Okay," I said after a moment, "But I'll repay you someday for this."

"You bet you will, boss." Charles smiled slyly.

I took the bucket and put it carefully onto the floor of the truck cab and then went back around to get in.

"One thing, Rick. Tran say, no matter what, do not put hands into bucket. You understand?"

"Yes," I said, "I understand."

That evening, after dinner, I told my wife about Plan C.

"You've lost your mind. You've finally lost your mind, haven't you?"

I knew I had an ace in the hole—Lynn is nuts over animals. I've never seen an animal that my wife didn't love. "Just come outside and have a look at them. They're beautiful fish. I think you'll like them."

"Like them!" she cried. "These are flesh eating monsters we're talking about, and you're going to use them as a weapon to exact revenge on some poor dumb animals. Rick, you really have lost it this time." I remember that for just a split second, just a nanosecond, I actually considered what she said. Nah, I thought, this'll work.

"Lynn, you really don't get it, do you? I didn't go to all of this trouble and expense just to sick a couple of fish on an unsuspecting varmint for cheap thrills. What kind of person do you think I am? The piranhas are for protection. They'll keep the raccoons out of the yard, keep them away from our dog and our cats. And they'll be our pets. Totally, ah, symbiotic, and nobody gets hurt. Just come out and meet them will you? Please."

Lynn named the couple Lucy and Desi. She helped me get them into their new, watery home and then we lifted the wire mesh over the water and I fastened it down to the redwood planks.

"I don't get this," my wife said. "How are the piranhas going to ward off the raccoons with this wire over the tank?

"Lucy and Desi need to be trained first. I read how to do it on the Internet. You'll see, in a couple weeks they'll be regular "watch fish".

On the way home from work the next evening, I stopped at our neighborhood butcher and bought a pound of flank steak. That night after dinner I cut off a little piece of the beef, tied one end to a three-foot string and went out to the patio. I lifted the wire mesh off the tank and peered in. No Lucy and Desi in sight, but I knew they were in there. I dropped the piece of meat into one end of the tank and then, using the string, I skimmed it quickly across the water to the other end, jerking as it went, simulating not too convincingly the 'frenzied and panic-like activity of victims'. Then back to the other end of the tank, allowing the meat to sink no more than a couple of inches into the water. I did this for about ten minutes. No site of the piranhas.

"Okay kids," I said, replacing the mesh over the tank and fastening it down, "no dinner for you two tonight."

The web article I'd read said that it could take up to a week before the piranhas would go for the meat the first time. Lucy and Desi went for it on the fourth night. Whack! When I pulled the meat out of the water, I saw a perfectly shaped crescent cut out of it. One more pass and the whole piece of flank steak was gone. The idea was to teach the fish to go for food that moved through the water quickly and with a jerking movement. Feeding piranhas other fish wouldn't work….they'd get into a hunting mentality that way. You wanted piranhas to strike instinctively and instantly, the moment they perceived movement.

I worked with Lucy and Desi for three weeks. By the end of the second week they were deadly quick and deadly accurate with their flank steak attacks. The string barely hit the water before the meat was gone. In fact, the string started getting shorter. Each night I made sure to place the mesh back over the tank. Didn't want any marauding coons to come down into the yard and meet the kids before they were ready for visitors.

It was nine years, nearly to the day, that we'd had the pond party back in September of 1991. It was a warm, balmy evening. Lynn had headed upstairs to bed. I went out to check the tank. Lucy and Desi were no longer standoffish toward me. Instead of hiding in the shadows, they approached the surface of the water when they saw me walk up. Flank steak time!

"No, you two," I said in a hushed voice, "you've gotten all you'll get from me tonight. But, hey, who knows, there might just be a little snack for you later." And with that I lifted off the wire mesh and set it aside. "Good night, Lucy. Good night Desi."

By all indications, Plan C worked. The next morning there was clear evidence that multiple raccoons had paid a visit. As before, the water lilies had all been removed from the water and strewn on the ground. But instead of fish skeletons and muddy little raccoon prints on the brick patio, there were bloody little raccoon prints, maybe four sets, everywhere and they led off up onto the hillside.

When Lucy and Desi saw me walk up, they surfaced looking for breakfast. Flank steak all around.

We lived in the house on Chula Vista for another year and a half. In that time we never saw a raccoon or found any evidence whatever that one had been in our yard. Several times I came close to stopping by Hecker Feed and Farm Supply, just to bring Mrs. Hecker a little closure, but I thought better of it. The fewer people who knew about Plan C, the better.

Why I Type So Fast
December 2003

I'm a terrific typist. One hundred-plus words a minute with few mistakes, and the mistakes I do make have more to do with poor spelling skills than with typing. The fact is, I can type faster than I can talk. And I owe it all to my high school biology teacher, Mr. Pitman, and a gopher I called Alice. Let me explain.

I was not a good student in high school, but I knew I wanted to go to college. My counselor, Mr. Thornton, gently encouraged me to explore options in the trades, "just as a back-up". My mom and dad weren't sure what I should do when I graduated high school, but they were pretty sure it shouldn't be to go to college. My father never really trusted people with a college degree. "Get a job and join a good union," he'd say, "and you'll be set." I was the only person who thought I was college material—it was like I was this brilliant person trapped inside the body of a C-minus student. So I insisted on taking college prep courses. What could

Mr. Thornton say? You're an idiot? You'll flunk out? Learn to weld like your dad?

So in my junior year at Hayward High School I got the biology class I asked for. There were two biology teachers at the school, Mr. Pitman, a gentle, quiet nerdy guy with an over-grown Jack Web crew cut and horned rimmed glasses who'd taught at Hayward High since the beginning of time; and Miss Breed, a short, stocky lifer with close cropped, salt and pepper hair and a humorless scowl with which she'd surely been born. Both were the perpetual wearers of white lab coats. I got Mr. Pitman.

I wasn't particularly worried about doing well in biology, which was my second mistake, my first enrolling in the class to begin with. By the end of the first month I was already foundering and Mr. Pitman was already aware that there was a problem. It was obvious he wanted me to succeed. He told me privately that he thought once we started doing labs I'd get into the swing of things. So when on one Friday, near the end of the period, Mr. Pitman announced that the following Monday we'd get to work with frogs, I was excited. We listened as our teacher, dressed in his starched white lab coat, told us what to expect. Mr. Pitman had a funny way of talking….he would end every third or fourth sentence with a sigh and a little smile and then go on talking.

"We will be investigating the contraction of the skeletal muscle of the frog's leg. The principle we will address is that of a single stimulus to a muscle which produces a simple twitch. The twitch is significant for study because it is this type of single contraction from which all normal body contractions are built." Mr. Pitman sighed and smiled. "The force exerted by the twitch is determined by the number of motor units (a neuron and its muscle cells) responding at the same time. Increasing the voltage used to stimulate the muscle will increase the number of motor units contracting at the same time. This is referred to as multiple motor unit summation." Another sigh and smile.

I felt encouraged. I was actually getting some of this. We were going to make a frog's leg twitch. I didn't exactly understand why, but that didn't especially bother me. Next Mr. Pitman told us about pithing (a brand new word for me) and muscle preparation. "The tool used for pithing the frog and preparing the frog gastrocnemius muscle is this." He held up what looked like a dowel with a needle stuck to one end, which, when I later got my hands on one, turned out to be exactly what it was. "The object of the pithing operation is to destroy specified parts of the central nervous system. In this case the frog is pithed as a means of immobilization and anesthesia. (Sigh) Generally, pithing the spinal cord only is adequate." (Smile) Some of the girls in the class squirmed in their seats, while the macho boys looked eager and ready to pith. One kid groaned, "Wow, this is cool. We gotta wait till Monday? Let's do it now." Mr. Pitman sighed and smiled. "Yes, Monday will be the day, class. Your lab coats and frogs will be all ready for you on Monday."

So this was it. Mr. Pitman had told me he thought I'd do well in lab, and this was going to be my chance to prove him right. That night at home I obsessed about the pithing experiment, trying to imagine each step. I even tried looking frog pithing up in the encyclopedia, but no luck. I think I even dreamt about frog legs, and then the next morning the idea came to me. (The brilliant me, not the C-minus student in whose body I was trapped.) If contraction of the skeletal muscles of a frog (a mere amphibian) was a big deal, how much better would the contraction of a mammal's muscle be? A LOT BETTER, I reasoned.

My mother's name was Millie. Millie felt about the plants in her garden the way most mothers feel about their children. She nurtured them with plant food and supplements and love and she protected them from their enemies. At least she tried. Of late she'd been fighting a losing battle with a gopher, so when I informed my mother that Saturday morning that I would dedicate my entire weekend to "getting that damned gopher", Millie was thrilled. I suppose she was a little suspicious too, but mostly she was glad that I was finally taking an interest in the yard. My mother suggested several strategies for doing the gopher in—she was a farm girl and had been around the track more than a few times when it came to killing what she called "varmants". When I told her I wanted to catch the gopher alive, she sent me to the hardware store for a live catch trap. And no, Millie didn't ask me why I wanted to catch the gopher live. I don't think she wanted to know.

By late Sunday afternoon I had my gopher. I guess I didn't really know what to expect; it was smaller than I thought a gopher would be, and lighter in color. For whatever reason, I just assumed it was a she and immediately dubbed the gopher Alice, after my aunt Alice. I poked some holes into the top of a shoe box, put Alice in there with a carrot and a piece of celery, and fastened the lid down with a piece of duct tape. That night I lay awake thinking about school the next day….generally I didn't look forward to going to school on Monday mornings (or any mornings), but this time it was different. I was going to earn my first A in biology.

The next day Alice spent the first three periods in her shoe box at the bottom of my locker. I checked on her before going to lunch—she hadn't touched the celery, but she'd worked on the carrot a little. I gave her some water in a little juice bottle cap. I don't quite know how to explain this, but I felt somehow grateful to the gopher. I wanted her last few hours to be comfortable. I felt no malice towards Alice. And I remembered what Mr. Pitman had said the Friday before: "…..the frog is pithed as a means of immobilization and anesthesia."

I arrived to biology class a little early that day and stowed the shoebox under the lab table on the floor. My plan was simple—I would substitute Alice for the frog Mr. Pitman would give me, follow all of the instructions for the experiment, and document the results, which I assumed would be different enough from everyone else's in the class to earn me an A for the lab session. Did I mention that I was an idiot in the eleventh grade?

It's difficult to describe what happened next…..it all happened so fast. I pulled the duct tape off the shoebox, grabbed Alice and held her firmly and inserted the dowel-needle device just below the bottom of her little rodent skull….the precise pithing spot shown in the mimeographed diagram each of us had been given. From the instant the needle entered Alice, it was evident that the second of the two purposes of pithing, that of 'anesthetizing the subject' had not been achieved to any ascertainable degree. What it did do was to cause an unbelievable gushing of Alice's blood as she squirmed out of my grasp. The classroom went crazy. Girls were screaming, boys were chasing the gopher up one aisle and down the next and Mr. Pitman was banging his pointer on the top of his desk and saying, almost to himself, "People….people….. people". The girl who sat in front of me, the prettiest girl in the class, in fact, one of the prettiest in the entire school, glared at me. "I hope you're satisfied," she hissed. She'd seen the whole thing, knew the gopher was my gopher, and worst of all, she knew what I'd planned to do with it. (The lovely Claudia Davenport would later become my wife and the mother of my two sons and I've often wondered if the Alice incident hadn't gotten us started off on the wrong foot.)

It was a long Monday afternoon. After being told that Mr. Pitman wished "never to see the Cornish boy again—ever", the Dean of Boys, Mr. Ochoa, explained to my mother (who'd been called at work to take part in the 'suspension meeting') that the only class available for me after lunch period was typing. So the following Thursday (Tuesday and Wednesday were, how shall I say, "leave without pay" days from school) I reported to Mrs. Hagen's Typing 1-A class. Twenty-three girls and me. Mrs. Hagen, and I'm sure the entire Hayward High faculty, had heard about the gopher incident and each day when I entered the classroom she did a full visual body search of me. It was a long year.

My game plan was to wait till my senior year and then sign up for biology again, this time with Miss Breed who, now in her forty-second year of teaching, had clearly lost all patience with high school-aged humankind. However, during the summer between the 11th and 12th grade, she and the school's most popular girl's gym teacher, Miss Heffenbok, had taken a week-long vacation together on Catalina Island, were spotted strolling on the beach hand-in-hand by Dr. Longnecker, our high school principal who, as luck would have it, was also vacationing on the Island, and were both immediately discharged, leaving only one biology teacher at Hayward High--Mr. Pitman. This time I lasted less than a week; although Mr. P was a gentle and kind man, it turned out he was also a holder of grudges. He'd said a year before he never wanted to see the Cornish boy again and, by God, he meant it. I re-enrolled in Typing 1-A again in my senior year, (they didn't have a 1-B) and by June I typed as fast as the wind. So as fate would have it, over the long haul learning to type served me way, way better than learning how to pith frogs.

The Nancy Waiver
November 2003

I'd taken a friend to the Humane Society in Santa Clara; she'd rounded up about a half dozen feral kittens in her neighborhood and was hoping she could find them a home. As I stood waiting around for my friend to do her business at the front counter, I wandered into the Lost Cat room. I'm not a huge cat lover—or even a liker for that matter—but I was just sort of killing time. As I walked by each cage peering in at the captives one by one, a yellow and white tabby locked eyes with me. PLEASE, PLEASE, PLEASE GET ME THE HELL OUT OF HERE. PLEASE. THEY'RE GOING TO KILL ME TODAY! It was as though the cat was screaming the words at me, but with just her eyes. I read the note clipped to her cage. Yep, she was due to be put down that day.

I went home and told Lynn about the telepathic episode and she, being the huge cat person that I am not, naturally concluded we had to adopt the cat, and right away. Pointing out that we already had three cats didn't seem to carry much weight. Neither did reminding her that I didn't even like cats, or that it was probably too late anyhow. My wife told me to call the Humane Society and tell them we were on the way and, as is my custom, I obeyed.

Half hour later we were seated in the office of the "Animal Adoption Coordinator." After filling out three pages of forms, which required both our signatures, we were given an addendum to sign.

"This is necessary," the Animal Adoption Coordinator explained, "because the adoptee, the cat in question, has been de-clawed. You must sign a witnessed stipulation that at no time will you allow the cat out doors. And that you will keep all doors and windows and other means of escape closed to prevent the cat from exiting the dwelling."

"But that's impossible", I said, "we have three other cats and two dogs and all of these animals spend time out of doors. We've got a doggie door for the dogs and open windows for the cats…these are in door/out door kind of pets. And they like it that way."

The Animal Adoption Coordinator arched his eyebrows and sighed. "I don't think you understand, Mr. Cornish. This feline has been de-clawed. She has no means of protecting herself. Outside in the elements the cat would be defenseless, probably killed within a few days. It must be kept in-doors. This is Humane Society policy."

So the Animal Adoption Coordinator and I argued for a while. I could tell Lynn was starting to come undone. She'd already named the cat. Nancy. Actually, Nancy Ann. I tried reasoning. I tried pleading. Finally I took a different tack.

"Okay," I said, "let me re-cap where I think we are. The 'cat in question' is scheduled to be killed today, right?"

"Euthanized, yes", said the Animal Adoption Coordinator.

"And unless we sign an agreement to keep all of the doors and windows of our house closed at all times, you won't give us the cat, right?"

"A witnessed stipulation, yes".

"And you'll kill her today, right?"

"Euthanize."

"Yes, euthanize. And that's Humane Society policy. H-U-M-A-N-E Society policy. Right?"

"Right."

"Okay then, " I said calmly and very, very agreeably, "I'd like to speak with the H-U-M-A-N-E Society person-in-charge."

Without speaking the Animal Adoption Coordinator got up from his chair and left the room. He was gone a long time. When he returned he was carrying the cat in question. He handed her to Lynn.

Nancy Ann came home with us in 1990. Lord only knows how old she is now. But she still gets around, and she seems happy enough. She's never tried talking to me again, telepathically or otherwise. Guess she figures there's never been another good reason to.

Cornish Miners
December 2003

My son Phillip arrived on Thanksgiving Day with another of his get rich quick schemes. He and his brother and I would pan for gold in Whiskey Creek and split all proceeds three ways. Cynic Peter balked at the idea until I pointed out that fortune hunting in our own backyard was light years more promising than Phil's scheme last Thanksgiving—a rent-a-Christmas-tree business. "Besides," I said, "what have we got to lose?" A once stung, twice wise kind of kid, Peter replied, "I don't know, but I'm sure we'll find out tomorrow morning."

And so the very first thing next morning we headed down to Jamestown where, nestled in between antique stores and bed and breakfasts, right there on Main Street, we found the Jamestown Prospecting Tours and Outfitters Company. Though the JPTOC makes far more money selling postcards and chunks of fools gold to tourists, they do carry a nice line of gold pans, how-to-find-gold books and maps of the more likely spots for finding the yellow stuff.

"Wow," said Phil, "check this out! Whiskey Creek!" Sure enough, there on a six fold glossy map of Tuolumne County was Whiskey Creek—my Whiskey Creek, the creek that runs through the middle of our six acres—and there right next to the crooked line on the map were three little miner's pick axes. "And that's out of a possible four", Phillip enthused. I suddenly found myself getting just a little excited when son number two reminded us both that we were not looking at a just-discovered treasure map. We were looking at a brochure cunningly designed to cause tourists to buy merchandize, and lots of it. Phillip and Peter disagreed over which type of gold pan to buy—one had a solid bottom and the other, fine wire screening—so, having well over twenty-five years experience as peace-maker in our little tribe, I bought both and we headed back home.

Edward and Lemuel Cubbage, two brothers from the tiny mining town of Redruth in the North of Cornwall, sailed from Port Gaverne on March 14, 1856. Since hearing of the gold find in California that sent shock waves around the world, the two brothers, both veteran tin miners in their mid-twenties, had saved every penny they could scrape together for the trip to the new world. The ocean voyage lasted just under two months and took them across the stormy Atlantic, down around the tip of South America known as Cape Horn and then close along the Pacific coast up to San Francisco. Judging from a diary found in the attic of the house the brothers eventually built and which still stands today adjacent to my property, the journey was not a comfortable one. "So sick were we when the boat began to roll and tumble that Will and me prayed to God that He might carry us home to Him. And thus whole days passed but in His perfect wisdom the Lord knew best and did deliver us." The two young Cornish miners landed in San Francisco on May 11, 1856, spent the last of their precious savings on prospecting equipment, provisions and a donkey, and within forty-eight hours of arriving in America, headed east toward the Sierras and their fortune.

Since Whiskey Creek runs December through May it was decided that we'd need an artificial source of water to use our new gold pans. I patched together three garden hoses, Phillip gathered together a pick and a couple spades and Peter went inside to see if the NBA was on yet. The creek stretches approximately two hundred yards across my property. The slope down to the creek from the house is a gentle one, but just across the creek, the hillside banks up steeply. Oaks and bays canopy the entire creek side and carry thickly all the way up to the ridgeline, which is also my property line. Even with the limitation imposed by the length of the hose we were using, the exact spot where we would start our prospecting was open for debate. And debate is what my two sons did, (and have done their entire lives) in earnest. Each had a theory about where the gold was most likely to be found. The theories were mutually exclusive. I stood and listened.

It was the last week in May that Edward and Lemuel Cubbage first set eyes on Whiskey Creek. They'd spent the night before at the Willows Hotel in Jamestown, the first real beds they'd slept in since their sea voyage, and had intended to head north up to Angel's Camp and beyond. But just a few miles outside of Jamestown, along a trail that would later become Shaw's Flat

Road, Will had gone up ahead of his brother, who was leading the donkey. When he came rushing back Will announced with a yelp that he'd found a likely spot—a slow, meandering stream with a gradual drop and deposits of quartz along either side. That night the Cubbage brothers camped along side of Whiskey Creek, no doubt within sight of where I sit this very moment.

"Whooooa, check this out." Phil was holding a tiny pebble, the size of a BB. Peter and I rushed over.

"It's not shiny," Peter said, "to be gold it's got to be shiny."

"It's yellow isn't it? Maybe it just needs to be polished. Here, put it in your mouth and bite down on it." We'd seen a photograph back at the Jamestown Prospecting Tours and Outfitters Company of Michael Landon biting a nugget of gold. The caption read, "Little Joe Discovers Gold in Jamestown".

"YOU bite down on it," Peter said, backing away.

"Here, give it to me," I said, still the peacemaker. I bit down hard on the rock and it disintegrated in my mouth. It was bitter. "Not gold," I said, spitting. "Hey," said Peter, "I think Chicago's playing New York. The two Cornish boys dropped their gold prospecting gear and walked up toward the house. As quickly as they'd begun, they ended their careers as gold prospectors.

But Edward and Lemuel Cubbage did find gold in Whiskey Creek. Lots of it. They staked a claim, twenty acres, and immediately began working the land for ore. But there was trouble from the beginning. Edward, the oldest brother, believed that the most lucrative approach for extracting the gold was to set up a sluice box and mine the creek. Lemuel was convinced that a shaft needed to be dug on the far side of the creek; he was sure that a rich vein would be found without having to dig too deep. After trying in vain to change one another's mind, the two Cornish miners went forward with their own separate plans and worked independently from that point on.

Along with Lemuel's diary, several yellow stained assayers receipts were found in the attic of the wood frame house the brothers built. The documents showed that within a few months of working their claim, the Cuggage brothers were taking into the Jamestown assay office a fair amount of dust and nuggets, some weeks as much as five hundred dollars worth. A lot of money in those days. Of course the records found in the attic didn't say whether the gold was coming from the creek or the shaft being dug in the side of the hill or both. But one thing was certain, the feud between the tin miners from Cornwall over the best way to pull gold from the claim continued. In fact, it continued over the next three years.

By the time I put away the tools, including my twenty-eight dollars worth of new strike-it-rich gear, rolled up the garden hoses and hiked back up to the house, my two sons were deeply immersed in basketball. One had the Bulls, the other the Nicks, and the competition both on screen and off was fierce. Then the buzzer announced half time.

"Come on boys," I said, "let's go get some lunch at the Willows."

The Willows Steakhouse is on the far north end of Main Street in Jamestown. Out front there's a weatherworn plaque that recounts the old clapboard structure's history: "In continual operation since 1851 as a hotel-boarding house-bar-restaurant-brothel, alternating uses depending on the shifting periods of lawlessness and peace-ability". Once inside the foyer, you can go left into the dining room or right into the bar. We went right. The room was dimly lit and furnished in 19th century saloon. Several large framed collections of news clippings hung on the walls, each telling a story about the Willows from some distant time. We sat under one and a waitress came over with menus and we ordered beers.

"Have I ever told you boys the story of the Cubbage brothers?" I asked?

"Oh, boy," said Phil, "here comes a good one." "A whopper," Pete groaned.

My sons had every right to be a little skeptical. Phillip and Peter first became suspicious of my story telling when they were seven and five respectively and I convinced them that our black Lab, Eddy, was actually a little person dressed in a fur costume…. they spent an hour one Saturday morning looking for his zipper.

"No seriously," I said, "I have a story to tell you, a true story, and I brought you here to tell it."

"Why here", asked Phil.

"Because here's where the story ends." This piqued their curiosity. And so I proceeded to tell my sons the tale of the brothers from Cornwall, the two young Cornish miners. About their dream of gold and fortune in the New World, their sea voyage, their stopover on the Barbary Coast, about their discovery of gold at Whiskey Creek, and about their years-long argument.

"You know the mounds that line some parts of the creek? Phil, you were sitting on one today. Well, those aren't natural mounds. If you dig through the thin layer of dirt and leaves, you'll find that they're actually piles of tailings—rocks thrown out of the creek during the sluicing process."

"So what happened to the brothers," Peter asked. "Did they get rich? Did they ever quit their feuding?"

"Yes," I said. "The feud ended right here. In this very room. Edward and Lemuel had worked their gold stake for about three years, and one Saturday evening, in the summer of 1861, they decided to ride into town, on the same road we just traveled, to have dinner."

"Here at the Willows," said Phil. Both boys were now clearly into the story.

"Here at the Willows," I said, "but then it was also a hotel, gambling den and house of ill repute. After dinner Edward and Lemuel got into a poker game. Who knows, maybe right here at this table. They were both drinking whiskey, and at some point in the game, they started in on their three-year argument about the best way to mine their property. Sluice the creek, dig a shaft. SLUICE THE CREEK! DIG A SHAFT! The argument heated up, more whiskey was drunk, and the brothers were egged on by the onlookers who were up for watching a good Saturday night fight. Suddenly words were replaced by fists, and then fists by knives, and before anyone could fully take in what was happening, it was all over.

The Cubbage Brothers from Cornwall had killed one another and they lay dead on the floor. This floor."

Phillip and Peter looked at one another, and then at me.

"That was a crock," said Peter. "Total BS," Phil chimed in.

"Really?" I said. "Read the newspaper behind you." They both stood up and turned to read the article, framed and under glass, hanging on the wall. The piece was dated November 15, 1972, and it's headline read "Willows Patrons Report Brothers on Prowl Again". The Union Democrat article was a color piece and told of two tourists, a man and his wife from the Bay Area, who reported seeing the ghosts of the Cubbage brothers. The article went on to tell the story of the two brothers, their immigration, their gold strike and their fateful feud that ended in the bar of the Willows. "At least ten times since the turn of the century," the article concluded, "this newspaper has reported sightings of Edward and Lemuel Cubbage. The Willows Steakhouse and Saloon is just one of many historical and colorful destinations which makes Jamestown a favorite of visitors to the Mother Lode."

I looked at my two sons and, for just a brief instant, I could see in their eyes that same look of wonder they'd had as they searched for the black Lab's zipper.

The Rescue of Albirdio
September 2005

Once, when my youngest son Peter was just a little guy, he was playing ball inside the house and broke a window. I'd been out in my shop and didn't hear the crash and Peter, not wanting to deal with the situation, just skipped over to a friend's house to play. When I found the broken window a while later and confronted my son, he readily admitted to being the culprit but didn't see as how he'd been the least bit dishonest by not telling me about it. I remember so vividly sitting him down and explaining, slowly and methodically about "lies of omission". I was adamant that having a truth and withholding it was just as serious an offense as telling a lie. It was as much a sermon as an explanation--I was that convicted by what I was saying. Peter got it. His brother Phillip, who'd been listening, got it too. We were all on the same page—you don't hold back information when you know it's important. Period.

Now let me tell you the story of our parrot's escape and rescue.

The story actually starts about six years ago. The evening dishes are done and my wife and I are sitting in front of the TV watching NOVA-- a one hour special on birds…..parrots specifically. Big ones, little ones, caged, wild. Mid way through the show we're introduced to Alex, the famous African Grey parrot at the University of Arizona's Department of Ecology and Evolutionary Biology. Dr. Irene Pepperberg has taught this bird to communicate, actually to read, and as Lynn and I watch we're mesmerized by the intelligence of this tiny creature. The narrator tells us that Alex (Avian Language Experiment) has the IQ of a two-year-old child. Amazing.

The next morning Lynn and I exchange e-mails from our respective offices at work.

Me: Hey, what did you think of those parrots last night? Pretty incredible. Ever thought you'd like to have a parrot for a pet.

She: No. We have all the pets we (which actually means ME because I take care of them) can handle.

Me: Ah, come on now, admit it. Wouldn't it be cool to have one of those African Greys? "It'll be more like having a little feathered friend than another pet. How hard could it be to take care of a little bird? I'll bet they don't eat much.

She: No more pets, Rick. Not even little feathered ones. No.

I backed off, but that was just the first volley. My wife loved animals and I knew she would get a kick out of owning an African Grey parrot; I just had to help her realize it. This took a week and a half. On the way home from the breeder, (a woman whose life was so obviously and completely interwoven with the lives of her birds that it should have given me some pause), we named the bird Albert. It was just a little bit of a thing, maybe two-thirds of its adult size, but by the time we pulled into our driveway the parrot had pierced me on the finger and on the wrist with its beak, drawing blood in both places. (With parrots, which have needle sharp beaks that can achieve 2000 psi (pounds of pressure per square inch), the word is "pierce", not bite.) The parrot didn't pierce Lynn at all, though he had plenty of chances. I remember thinking that was a little odd.

And so began what slowly and inexorably grew into one of the truly dark periods of my life. I say slowly because the bond between Lynn and the parrot didn't form overnight. Nor did the bird's obsessive, all-consuming hatred of me. Days turned into weeks and I still found myself amused by his antics. Weeks turned to months and amusement turned to indifference. Gradually the bird began imitating birds he would hear out in the yard. Jays, mocking birds, doves. He did doves so realistically that sometimes they would coo back to him. Then, roughly six months after Albert moved in, he began to talk. The darkness began to settle in quickly from there. His first word was Doh, ala Homer Simpson. The next word was Albirdio. Yes, the African Grey parrot had renamed himself. It was chilling….I remembered with smothering irony what I'd said to Lynn six months ealier….'It'll be more like having a little feathered friend than another pet.'

I began to fully grasp the magnitude of what lay in store for our household a couple months after Albirdio began talking. I was in the kitchen preparing the evening meal when I suddenly heard a commotion in the family room. As I rushed in, I saw our dog,

Alex, running in circles around the room, knocking over a lamp, up-ending an end table, and barking hysterically. And there, on his perch, safely above the fray, was the African Grey parrot, repeating, in precisely my voice, over and over, "Alex, do you wanna go for a walk? Alex, do you wanna go for a walk?" And there, standing in the threshold of the family room, I remembered what the MIT researcher had said—African Grey parrots have the intellect of a two year old child. And then in a sudden rush, I remembered every unpleasant experience I'd ever had with a toddler.....two to three year old humans whose universe revolves solely around them, who have not yet learned right from wrong, whose happiness depends entirely on pushing the buttons of those around them. And I realized with a dark shudder that Albirdio was intellectually a toddler and that he would remain a toddler for his entire parrot life, which could last as long as eighty-five years. This sociopath, this relentless pusher of buttons, this ruthless piercer of human flesh, would out live me.

A few months later, in the middle of the night, one of the smoke detectors downstairs went off. I got up groggily, went down stairs and found that, rather than a fire, we had a detector in the family room with a failing battery. I got a ladder, replaced the battery and went back to bed. (The alarm couldn't have been on for more than 30 seconds.) Two nights later, again in the middle of the night, the smoke detector went off again. But this time, as soon as I turned on the lights downstairs, the detector went silent. I found the ladder and checked out the alarm. The battery looked fine. The connection seemed okay. I went back to bed. No sooner had I fallen asleep than the alarm went off again. This time when I trundled back down stairs I didn't turn the light on immediately.... instead, I listened to the sound of the alarm. It wasn't coming from the family room's smoke detector at all; it was coming from the bird's room, which didn't have a smoke detector. I shuddered. It had taken less than thirty seconds for Albirdio to memorize the sound of the smoke detector alarm two nights before, less than thirty seconds to master yet another one of my buttons.

In the months that followed Albirdio taught himself many other sounds, all of which had one thing in common….each sound possessed the power to "activate" me. I'd be outside and the phone would ring inside. We'd be watching TV and the doorbell would ring. Eventually he even got Lynn's voice down…."Hey, Rick"…. and I'd go from upstairs to downstairs, downstairs to upstairs.

All the while the parrot was honing his sadistic skill sets, he was getting closer and closer to my wife. Albirdio loved her. She loved the bird, bought him the best of everything….toys, cage, food. They would coo at each other…..sometimes he would even regurgitate his food for her—the ultimate show of affection from a bird. And over time they developed their rituals. When Lynn would shower and put on her makeup in the morning, they would call to one another, have what seemed like conversations, sing songs together—Jingle Bells was their favorite, she singing the words, Jingle bells, jingle bells, jingle all the way, he doing his chicken imitation, Cluck cluck cluck, cluck cluck cluck, cluck cluck cluck cluck cluck. Later, before leaving for work, Lynn and the bird would prepare his breakfast in the kitchen—the freshest of fruits and vegetables, but also cheese and pasta, basically anything he showed a fancy to. On the weekends the parrot would ride around on her shoulder as she did her housework mimicking the sound of the vacuum cleaner.

When I complained about her bird, Lynn would explain patiently, as if to a child, that he was just a tiny, innocent little bird, less than twelve ounces, she would say. I was a grown man, an adult, surely I could accept his "little birdie nature". And then, for good measure…."Remember, it was you and not me who wanted this bird. Now that he's my bird, I have a commitment to him. A lifetime commitment. Learn to live with it."

A turning point for the parrot and I came in the winter of 2000. Lynn's father, Tony, died and my wife flew back to New York for the funeral. I was left in charge of taking care of the animals—the two dogs, the three cats, the four fish and the African Grey parrot. The first several days the bird was okay….in fact, better than okay since he'd stopped talking and chirping the morning that Lynn left. He seemed depressed. But somehow it was like he knew when it was time for Lynn to return home. The morning of her return Albirdio was as noisy as ever, and when I passed near his cage while vacuuming, he debuted a brand new insult….."You little f_ _ _ er" he said, and in my wife's voice. I naturally replied in kind, and then Albirdio repeated the epithet, this time louder and with feeling. I went on with my housecleaning. I wasn't going to argue with this bird.

Around noon it was time to feed the parrot and change his water….Lynn had left exacting instructions on what I was to serve him each day. After giving Albirdio his apple slices, seeds, slice of Swiss cheese, grapes, pasta (with Romano cheese), etc., etc., I reached in his cage to get his water dish. In a blur, he swooped down from his perch and caught the tip of my right index finger. The needle-sharp beak went in under the nail and came out at the cuticle. The nail peeled off. Blood spurted. "You little f_ _ _ er", said the African Grey Parrott.

I've told this story to many people, and a good number of them have asked what I did to the bird after he slashed my finger open. 'If I'd been you I'd have killed 'em' many have said. No, I always say, if you'd been me you wouldn't have killed the bird, because, if you'd been me, you'd have been married to Lynn and you wouldn't have laid a finger on him.

To say that the finger incident was hurtful to the relationship Albirdio and I shared would be like saying that Hitler's invasion of Poland caused a ripple of controversy in Europe. The battle lines had been drawn, and during the years that followed, it was a cold war, but a war nonetheless. As he grew into a mature living thing, Albirdio expressed his "little birdie nature" in more and more sophisticated ways….always finding new avenues for showing affection to Lynn, always looking for new tricks to show his feelings for me. For my part, I began to research African Greys on the Internet. Parrots, I learned, were the smartest of all birds, African Greys the smartest of all parrots. The smarter the animal, the greater chance of neurosis—true in birds, true in people. And Greys were one-person pets….the closer they grew to a single individual, the more antagonistic they became toward everyone else. Especially those with whom, in their twisted little birdie minds, they were in competition.

Then, in the fall of 2003, a miraculous and wonderous thing happened —Albirdio disappeared. It was a Sunday afternoon. A former employee of mine and her husband and two children stopped by in Jamestown to see us on their way home from a camping trip. We showed them around the property then sat in our family room and chatted for about an hour. The bird was unusually talkative that day—normally he says nothing when strangers are around but he was impatient that they leave. (Did I mention he hates all people except Lynn?) His cage door was open, as was Lynn's practice when we were home, but Albirdio stayed inside. When our friends announced they needed to be headed home, Lynn and I walked them out to the parking compound. The Grey was in his cage, with the door open, and when we walked out onto the deck and toward the compound, we left the French doors open…..as we had a thousand times before.

Ten minutes later when Lynn and I returned into the house, the bird was gone. Vanished. "Birdio, where are you? Birdio." Lynn went from room to room, calling. Then she went through the house a second time, still calling, "Birdio, where are you? Birdio" but now panic was beginning to well up in her voice.

For the next three hours we searched….the house, outside, back in the house, finally in stupid places, drawers, underneath the couch, behind the refrigerator. As night fell I laid out the possible scenarios as humanely as I could to my wife. The bird hopped out of his cage and: 1) was grabbed by one of the three cats—they were terribly frightened of the bird (as everyone but Lynn was) but maybe, just maybe, they'd finally had enough of Albirdio); 2) walked out the open door to the deck and was grabbed by a hawk or other bird of prey—there were certainly plenty around; or 3) walked out onto the deck and just flew away. The last scenario required that Albirdio's wings were grown back sufficiently since his last clipping. We didn't know whether that was the case; neither of us remembered when he'd last been clipped by the vet. But Lynn was betting on scenario three, and it upset her all the more because it meant that the bird would be somewhere out there in the dense forest just off the deck. A forest with hawks and owls and foxes and bobcats and coyotes and even an occasional mountain lion. Carnivores to whom an African Grey parrot, while not a filling meal, would surely be a tasty one.

Lynn bundled up and went out one more time that night with a flashlight. I sat there reading, feeling guilty for letting her go out alone, but knowing that if we couldn't find him in daylight, we sure weren't going to find him in the dark. That night she cried herself to sleep. As much as I hated the nasty, neurotic, vicious, ill-tempered parrot, I'd have given anything for him to suddenly re-appear unharmed. That's how much I love my wife.

The next day Lynn called me several times at work. Called to tell me he hadn't come home….that she'd ran an add in the paper….. posted a message on the community bulletin board, called the Humane Society. She sounded terrible. I didn't know what to expect when I came home from work that night. She and the dogs greeted me as I pulled into the parking compound….her eyes were red and swollen, but she forced a little smile. I could see she'd begun the process of getting through her loss. Before dinner we went out and hunted some, both knowing without admitting that we were now looking for the remains of Albirdio. After an hour, we went inside and didn't mention the bird the rest of the evening. The next day, about mid morning, I got a brief e-mail from Lynn.

--Please don't even think about getting me another bird. I'm finished with having a bird. This is just way, way too painful.—

We know each other so well. I had already begun thinking about another bird, maybe a Cockateel …..certainly not another African Grey. I was rid of the feathered, evil one.

That evening when I came home Lynn was doing better than the night before. "Shall we go out and look around for a while," I asked. "No," she said, "I've been out searching half the day. He's not out there. He's gone. I just hope he's not lost somewhere and can't get home. It breaks my heart to think of him lost and all alone." We went to bed early that night. Unlike most nights, Lynn fell asleep first. I'm sure she was exhausted by all the hoping and looking and worrying she'd been doing. Me, I couldn't fall asleep. I was feeling too excited at the thought of being a birdless family again….too satisfied with the events of the last couple days. Man, I had every right to feel great about the bird being gone. I was perfectly justified. No, I wasn't gloating, I was feeling exactly the way I should be feeling. And I hadn't done ANYTHING to cause this. Whatever happened to the bird, I had nothing to do with it. NOTHING TO DO WITH IT. My hands were clean.

But still I couldn't fall asleep. I got up, poured a glass of wine and went out on the deck and got comfortable on a recliner. There below me was our pasture, and beyond that, Whiskey Creek, and then the steep side of the canyon running up to the ridge and our property line. Totally canopied by towering oak trees, a forest, dark and beautiful and totally still. After just a sip of wine and the warm Indian summer night air, my eyes started to blink shut. Then suddenly, the sound of a far away dove. Then another. Coooo. My mind fought back to consciousness, eyes blinked open…. Coooo. And then it hit me--doves don't coo at night. Now I was totally awake. No, I thought, this can't be happening. Obviously, I mumbled to myself, SOME doves do coo at night. Coooo.

I got up suddenly. I need to go to bed, I thought. This is ridiculous, I'm beginning to hear things. I opened the door and had one foot in the house. "You little f_ _ _ _ er." It was so faint, so distant as to be almost no sound at all. Maybe, I thought, it wasn't.

A moment later, I was in bed with the covers pulled up. I was ready to go to sleep. Tired. Got to sleep. I closed my eyes and saw Albirdio, high up in a tree in the forest, lost and all alone. Like Lynn had said earlier, "lost and all alone." Good, I thought. Perfect place for him. Couldn't happen to a nicer parrot. And it's not my fault. Besides, the hateful little bundle of feathers is being digested right this very moment….in the stomach of one of the cats. Or maybe being shared by a mama hawk and all her chicks. I didn't hear anything out there. I couldn't have, the bird couldn't have lasted this long if it did fly off. And what if I did hear Albirdio in the forest? Who knows that I heard him? Nobody. I'm guiltless. Not my problem. I squeezed my eyes shut. Got to sleep. I have got to fall asleep……And then, from way, way back….so far back in my mind and in years it was as faint as Albirdio's profanity….I could hear the explanation to my little boy after he'd broken the window and not told me. Peter got it, he understood. Did I?

It took a 20-foot extension ladder, a 12-foot pruning pole, the help of one of our neighbors, three flashlights and a floodlight, rope, duct tape, a canoe paddle, a towel, and three hours to rescue the bird. Lynn had been right. Albirdio had flown into the forest and had gotten lost. It had flown across the pasture, down to the creek, up the other side to the ridgeline and then into a giant pine tree on our neighbor's property. We learned from Janice, our neighbor, that she'd seen him up in her tree the morning before last. So Albirdio had taken off, gotten lost, landed and just stayed put—that's' what had saved him. And somehow I'd heard him from a quarter of a mile away. And somehow in the dense oak and pine and scrub, among hundreds and hundreds of trees, Lynn had found him way up high sitting on a branch. "Doh", he'd said to her when she shined the flashlight up there. "Doh."

Lynn says that after his ordeal the bird's personality changed. He's sweeter, she says, gentler. I don't see it.

CPSIA information can be obtained at www.ICGtesting.com
Printed in the USA
BVOW030022190912

300802BV00001B/6/P